Post-Traumatic Stress Disorder

A Mind-Body Approach to Overcoming Traumatic Stress Symptoms and Recovering from Childhood Trauma

Sheila Redford

© Copyright 2020 by Sheila Redford - All rights reserved.

This document is geared towards providing exact and reliable information in regards to the topic and issue covered. The publication is sold with the idea that the publisher is not required to render accounting, officially permitted, or otherwise, qualified services. If advice is necessary, legal or professional, a practiced individual in the profession should be ordered.

- From a Declaration of Principles which was accepted and approved equally by a Committee of the American Bar Association and a Committee of Publishers and Associations.

In no way is it legal to reproduce, duplicate, or transmit any part of this document in either electronic means or in printed format. Recording of this publication is strictly prohibited and any storage of this document is not allowed unless with written permission from the publisher. All rights reserved.

The information provided herein is stated to be truthful and consistent, in that any liability, in terms of inattention or otherwise, by any usage or abuse of any policies, processes, or directions contained within is the solitary and utter responsibility of the recipient reader. Under no circumstances will any legal responsibility or blame be held against the publisher for any reparation, damages, or monetary loss due to the information herein, either directly or indirectly.

Respective authors own all copyrights not held by the publisher.

The information herein is offered for informational purposes solely, and is universal as so. The presentation of the information is without contract or any type of guarantee assurance.

The trademarks that are used are without any consent, and the publication of the trademark is without permission or backing by the trademark owner. All trademarks and brands within this book are for clarifying purposes only and are the owned by the owners themselves, not affiliated with this document.

Table of Contents:

INTRODUCTION — 1

CHAPTER 1: PTSD, IT'S CAUSES, SYMPTOMS AND EFFECTS — 3

1.1 Overview — 3

1.2 Symptoms — 4

1.3 Causes — 6

1.4 Effects — 8

CHAPTER 2: WHY PTSD CLASSIFIED AS AN ANXIETY DISORDER — 11

2.1 Generalized Anxiety Disorder [GAD] — 12

2.2 Anxiety Disorder — 13

2.3 Post-Traumatic Stress Disorder [PTSD] — 15

2.4 The Differences Between Panic Disorder and PTSD — 16

2.5 Understanding Generalized Anxiety Disorder (GAD) — 18

2.6 The Relationship between PTSD and GAD — 18

CHAPTER 3: STRESS MANAGEMENT & ITS TECHNIQUES — 20

3.1 What's the Stress? — 20

3.2 Effective Stress Management Techniques — 21

3.3 Tips for Stress Management — 24

3.4 Various Approaches and Methods for Stress Management — 25

CHAPTER 4: COPING WITH OVERTHINKING AND DEPRESSION — 28

4.1 Disorder of Overthinking-What's it? — 28

4.2 How to Stop Overthinking — 31

4.3 Overthinking and Anxiety — 33

4.4 Bipolar Disorder and Overthinking — 34

4.5 Mentally Strong People — 36

4.6 Hypochondria — 39

CHAPTER 5: PTSD COPING STRATEGIES — 42

5.1 Few Approaches to Consider — 42

5.2 The Use of Relaxation Exercises — 46

CHAPTER 6: DEALING WITH TRAUMA — 50

6.1 Trauma Defined — 50

6.2 Trauma Symptoms — 52

6.3 Modalities for Trauma — 52

6.4 What is Emotional and Psychological Trauma? — 53

6.5 Trauma Recovery Tips — 56

6.6 Healthy Ways to Cope with a Crisis — 62

CHAPTER 7: WAYS TO DEAL WITH VOLATILITY AND ANGER — 65

7.1 Understanding Anger: Explosive, Passive, Chronic — 65

7.2 5 Passive Rage Identification Methods — 66

7.3 Anger-Related Mental Disorders — 67

7.4 Chronic Anger — 69

7.5 Useful Things to Try — 70

7.6 Focus on Managing Yourself — 74

7.7 Anger Styles and Coping Strategies: — 77

CHAPTER 8: FORGETTING PAST TRAUMA AND ANXIETY — 82

8.1 Memories and Trauma — 82

8.2 How to Heal — 84

8.3 Forgetting Past — 85

8.4 Weakening Memories that Cause Phobia — 89

8.5 A Drug to be Forgotten? — 90

CHAPTER 9: RELAXATION TECHNIQUES — 92

9.1 Relaxation Technique 1 — 93

9.2 Relaxation Technique 2 — 94

9.3 Relaxation Technique 3 — 95

9.4 Relaxation Technique 4 — 96

9.5 Relaxation Technique 5 — 100

9.6 Relaxation Technique 6 — 101

CHAPTER 10: PTSD THERAPIES — 105

10.1 Self-Therapy — 105

10.2 Couples Self-Therapy — 107

10.3 Medication and Psychotherapy — 112

10.4 EMDR therapy — 115

CONCLUSION — 119

REFERENCES — 120

Introduction

Post-traumatic Stress Disorder (PTSD) is a persistent and sometimes crippling condition precipitated by psychologically overwhelming experience. It develops in a significant proportion of individuals exposed to trauma, and untreated, can continue for years. Its symptoms can affect every life domain – physiological, psychological, occupational, and social. Post-trauma stress reactions have been recognized throughout history. They are described in classical Greek literature and in the early literature of scientific medicine, but it was first diagnostically defined in modern times in the 1980 American Psychiatric Association Diagnostic and Statistical Manual. The surge of scientific and clinical interest in the condition over the past two decades has been largely due to awareness of problems associated with returning Vietnam combat veterans and advocacy by the feminist movement on behalf of rape victims. PTSD has not been documented in other groups including abused children, victims of crimes, accidents, and natural disasters. Not all trauma survivors develop PTSD. About 20% of crime victims, across type of crime, will meet diagnostic criteria. The rates are substantially higher for some crimes. For example, more than half of rape victims are afflicted. However, most crime victims do have some initial PTSD symptoms that subside over time.

Post-traumatic stress disorder is a mental health condition that is either felt or observed as a result of a traumatic experience. Symptoms can include hallucinations, visions, and severe anxiety, as well as uncontrollable thoughts about the incident. Some people who have been through traumatic incidents may have some issues with adjustment and coping, but now with time and a good self-care they typically get better. If the symptoms get worse, last months or even years, and disrupt in your social functioning, you may have PTSD.

Contrary to these attitudes, people with anxiety disorders are unable to cope. Disorders of anxiety often tend to highlight particular concerns and fears, like losing one's work for specific reasons. OCD is often related to obsessions with abstract concerns like germs, however. Following the APA's recommendation of excluding OCD from the list of anxiety disorders, it is often recognized or viewed by many mental health professionals as an anxiety disorder. For example, the Anxiety and Depression Association of America [ADAA] has a page dedicated to OCD.

We all experience stress in our lives. Because the large proportion of health problems are caused or affected by stress, it is important to recognize how stress affects your body and to practice successful stress management methods to make stress work for you instead of against you.

Relaxation techniques such as meditation, deep breathing, massage, or yoga can activate the body's relaxation response and ease symptoms of PTSD. Avoid alcohol and drugs. When you're struggling with difficult emotions and traumatic memories, you may be tempted to self-medicate with alcohol or drugs. So what are some things you can do, in addition to CBT and any other treatments recommended by your doctor, in order to keep your PTSD symptoms under control? Here are a few approaches you may want to consider.

Chapter 1: PTSD, it's Causes, Symptoms and Effects

1.1 Overview

Post-traumatic stress disorder is a state of mental health induced by a stressful event— either experiencing or watching it. Symptoms may include hallucinations, delusions, and severe anxiety, as well as the event's uncontrollable thoughts.

Most people who go through traumatic incidents may have some adjustment and coping problems, but they usually get better with time and good self-care. You may have PTSD if the symptoms get worse, last for months or even years, and interfere with your daily functioning.

During and after a traumatic situation, it is reasonable to be scared. Fear causes many of the body's split-second changes to help protect or avoid danger. This response to "fight-or-flight" is a typical response designed to protect a person from injury. Upon trauma, almost everyone will undergo a range of reactions, yet most people will naturally recover from the initial symptoms. PTSD can be treated to those who continue to experience problems. People with PTSD may feel stressed or afraid, even if they are not at risk.

Those with PTSD have serious, upsetting thoughts and feelings that have to do with their experiences that last long after the traumatic event is over. By flashbacks or hallucinations, they may recreate the game; they may feel sadness, fear, or anger; and they may feel disconnected or isolated from others. People with PTSD may avoid situations or individuals that remind them of the traumatic event and may have strong inauspicious reactions to something as ordinary as a loud noise or accidental touching.

PTSD treatment involves exposure to a traumatic event that is disturbing. Nevertheless, rather than the first-hand experience could be indirect. PTSD, for instance, may occur in a person hearing about a near family's violent death. It may also occur as a result of repeated exposure to traumatic trauma information such as police officers subjected to the knowledge of cases of child abuse.

1.2 Symptoms

Post-traumatic stress disorder (PTSD) symptoms can affect daily life dramatically.

In most cases, after a traumatic event, the symptoms progress during the first month.

But there might be months or even years before signs begin to appear in a minority of cases.

Some people with PTSD experience long duration when their signs are less noticeable, followed by periods of worsening. Some people have severe and persistent symptoms.

PTSD's specific symptoms can vary widely among individuals but generally fall within the categories listed below.

The most usual symptom of PTSD is re-experiencing.

This is when a person relives the traumatic event involuntarily and vividly in the form of flashbacks, hallucinations, recurring and distressing images or feelings, physical sensations such as discomfort, sweating, feeling sick, or trembling. Many people have constant negative thoughts about their experience, repeatedly asking themselves questions that prevent them from coming to terms with the case.

We might wonder why the event happened to them, for example, and whether they could have done anything to stop it, which could lead to feelings of guilt or shame.

The main symptom of PTSD is to try to avoid being conscious of the traumatic event.

Usually, this means avoiding other individuals or locations that remind you of the trauma or avoid talking about your experience to anyone.

Most people with PTSD are trying to push out of their minds reminders of the incident, sometimes distracting themselves with work or hobbies.

Most people try not to feel anything at all to cope with their emotions. This is referred to as mind-numbing.

This can cause the individual to become lonely and withdrawn, and they can also give up on the activities they used to enjoy.

Hyper arousal (feeling' on edge') Someone with PTSD might be very anxious and find relaxation difficult. We may be constantly aware of risks and be easily shocked.

This state of mind is referred to as hyper arousal.

Hyper arousal also leads to irritability, angry outbursts, sleeping difficulties (insomnia), trouble focusing on other issues. Most people with PTSD also have a variety of other concerns, including other mental health problems, such as depression, anxiety or phobia, self-harming, or destructive behavior, such as drug abuse or alcohol abuse. Other physical symptoms, such as headaches.

Post-traumatic symptoms of stress disorder can begin within one month of a traumatic event, but symptoms may not appear until years after the fact. Such signs cause significant difficulties in relationships and social or job conditions. They may also mess with your ability to do your usual day-to-day activities.

Symptoms of PTSD are commonly classified into four types: recurring thoughts, avoidance, negative thinking and mood changes, and changes in physical and emotional reactions. Over time, symptoms can differ or vary from person to person.

Intrusive memories Signs of intrusive memories may include, recurring unwelcome distressing thoughts of the traumatic event• Reflecting the traumatic event as if it were happening again (flashbacks). Updating the traumatic event's dreams or hallucinations • Severe emotional distress or physical reactions to something that reminds you of the traumatic event. You may have more signs of PTSD when you're profoundly depressed or when you have reminders of what you've been through. You can hear a car backfire, for example, and relive memories of battle. Or you might see a news report about a sexual assault and feel overwhelmed by your abuse memories.

1.3 Causes

When someone experiences post-traumatic stress disorder, terror, anxiety, and trauma memories last a long time and interfere with how they deal with daily life.

PTSD is caused by such a traumatic event— an event that may have been life-threatening or causing serious injury or sexual violence. Although a breakup or loss of a job relationship may feel traumatic, these are not the types of events that usually cause PTSD.

The kinds of experiences that could cause PTSD are:

- Serious accidents

- Natural disasters such as bushfires, floods, and earthquakes

- living in a war zone as a victim of war or as a soldier

- Sexual assault or threatened sexual assault

- Seeing people hurt or killed. Anyone may develop PTSD, but some people are at higher risk. The reasons for developing PTSD by some people while others are not fully understood. Probably there is a complex mix of ideas.

When you go through, or learn about an incident that involves actual or threatened death, serious injury, or sexual violation, you can develop post-traumatic stress disorder.

As with most mental health issues, PTSD is probably caused by a complex mix of • Stressful events, including the amount and extent of trauma you have endured in your life • Inherited mental health hazards, such as family history of anxiety and depression • Inherited personality traits — often referred to as your temperament • How the brain controls chemicals and hormones. While most people eventually adapt to the after-effects of such incidents, over time, some people find their symptoms worse. The result of PTSD is these deteriorating symptoms.

- Physicians cannot explain why some people develop PTSD, as is usually the case for mental health problems. Probable causes of PTSD, according to the Mayo Clinic, include inherited behavioral and personality traits, a combination of life experiences, and how the brain controls hormones and chemicals when responding to stress.

Risk factors Post-traumatic stress disorder can occur in people of all ages. Nevertheless, certain factors that make you more likely to develop PTSD after a traumatic event such as

- Experience intense or long-lasting trauma
- Having endured other earlier life trauma such as child abuse
- Having other health issues such as anxiety or anxiety.

1.4 Effects

Short-term and long-term symptoms of PTSD Post-traumatic stress disorder, according to the American Psychological Association (APA) and NCBI, induces short-term memory loss and may have long-term permanent psychological consequences. Luckily, psychotherapeutic intervention and treatment can alleviate PTSD's short-term and long-term effects and often eliminate them.

PTSD contains a range of symptoms that can affect members of the family. When someone has PTSD, they can have an impact on their ability to work as a parent or spouse, and changes in their functioning can lead to unmet family needs and increased family stress. This section provides information on the effects on families, children, and relationships of PTSD and trauma.

Families' • PTSD effects on PTSD families will make it difficult for someone to deal with. Living with someone who is easily frightened, has hallucinations and/or avoids social situations can take a toll on the most loving members of the family. PTSD research has demonstrated the harmful effect of PTSD on families.

- If the child's parent has PTSD A, the PTSD symptoms of the parent are directly related to the reactions of the child. The segment explains how the PTSD symptoms of caregivers affect children and discuss some of the common issues of PTSD faced by military children or other adults. The segment also includes guidance on how to tackle these challenges.

Trauma survivors may have difficulty maintaining their close family relationships or friendships with PTSD. PTSD symptoms can cause problems with confidence, closeness, communication, and problem-solving that, in effect, can influence how a loved one reacts to the survivor of the trauma.

• Relationships Learn about the circular pattern that can sometimes damage close family relationships may create.

Military families frequently contend with unusual stress cycles associated with deployments and may struggle to be able to cope with family changes or their loved ones deployed. This segment provides information to families who may have trouble with military deployments.

• Veterans' spouses with PTSD may have an effect on how couples get together. It can also have a direct effect on partners' mental health. This segment addresses common issues in marriages where one or both partners have PTSD and provides basic information on how to support couples with these issues.

• How deployment stress impacts families this segment discusses how it can be extremely challenging for a family to deploy a service member to a combat zone.

Post-traumatic stress disorder can affect your entire life— your career, your relationships, your wellbeing, and your daily pleasure.

Post-traumatic stress disorder may also increase your risk of other mental health issues such as • Depression and anxiety • Drug or alcohol use issues• Eating disorders• Suicidal thoughts and behavior

Chapter 2: Why PTSD Classified as an Anxiety Disorder

In the psychological community, there is a tradition of disagreement about how to identify different types of anxiety disorders. For decades before the publication of the fifth edition of the Mental Disorders Diagnostic and Statistical Manual [DSM-5] in 2013, the American Psychiatric Association [APA] listed the following under the broad anxiety disorder umbrella: generalized anxiety disorder [GAD], social anxiety disorder [SAD], panic disorder, and obsessive-compulsive disorder [OCD]. However, the anxiety disorder of DSM-5 removed the category of OCD and listed it together with other related disorders on its own.

Anxiety prevalence is still an OCD aspect, and this is recognized by the DSM-5. Nevertheless, the manual is more based on the variations.

"OCD's hallmark is a therapeutic dimension that is not usually present in anxiety disorders," said Anya Shumilina, a Therapeutic Associates owner, a center specializing in cognitive behavioral therapy. "Individuals diagnosed with OCD are known to drawn in strict compulsive and repetitive habits, such as turning lights on and off ten times before leaving home, to alleviate stress caused by compulsive thinking."

Contrarily, people with anxiety disorders are unable to cope with these behaviors. Anxiety disorders also tend to highlight specific concerns and fears, Shumilina said, including for specific reasons losing one's work. However, OCD is often associated with obsessions with vague fears such as germs.

Following the recommendation of the APA to exclude OCD from the list of anxiety disorders, many mental health professionals often recognize it or view it as an anxiety disorder. For instance, America's [ADAA] Anxiety and Depression Association has a page dedicated to OCD.

The division in the field of psychology may cause confusion, but there may be advantages under the umbrella of anxiety to continue treating OCD and other disorders. According to Dr. Shanthi, Director of Psychiatry at the Mountainside Treatment Facility, mental health professionals frequently ignore screening for conditions that are not technically anxiety disorders but have significant anxiety symptoms. These include OCD and [PTSD] post-traumatic stress. By including these disorders under the anxiety umbrella, people may have a greater chance of receiving the treatment they need. Luckily, therapies tend to be similar to anxiety disorders and OCD.

Many publications and associations on mental health also recognize PTSD as a condition of anxiety. The ADAA also has a page devoted to PTSD.

We made a comprehensive list of the different types of anxiety disorders to be both inclusive and attentive to the decision of the APA. Based on her professional experience and knowledge of DSM-5 anxiety disorders, we also included feedback from Andrea G. Batton, Ceo of the Maryland Anxiety Center.

2.1 Generalized Anxiety Disorder [GAD]

GAD is persistent and intense anxiety for anything. People with GAD are struggling to control their concerns. Despite a lack of evidence, they appear to expect some sort of disaster.

Social Anxiety Disorder

People have an intense fear of social anxiety disorder that others will evaluate them in social or performance circumstances. We are scared by the potential embarrassment or humiliation. The anxiety can be severe to the point where the desire to socialize, date, or fly is hindered.

According to a doctor, • 10 Signs You Have Social Anxiety • What Causes Social Anxiety?

SAD-related selective mutism in children is a condition of anxiety in which a child develops an ineptitude to speak in certain social settings such as school. According to the Selective Mutism, Anxiety, and Related Disorders Treatment Center, more than 90% of children with selective mutism also have social anxiety.

2.2 Anxiety Disorder

Panic disorder involves having panic attacks that arise spontaneously and come from nowhere. The attacks are so powerful that they create anxiety in the future to witness them.

Agoraphobia

Although the media perpetuates stereotypes, agoraphobia does not necessarily involve a fear of leaving home. Agoraphobia is a form of anxiety disorder where people fear and avoid places or circumstances that may cause them to panic or feel trapped, powerless, or humiliated. You are fearful of a real or expected scenario like using public transport, being in open or enclosed areas, standing in line, or being in crowds.

Agoraphobia also coincides with panic disorder, and they are classified together by many mental health organizations. For instance, if panic attacks occur in a particular location, the patient can avoid that location and develop agoraphobia. In extreme cases, the patient may experience as a space of distress anywhere outside his or her home.

Certain phobias People with specific phobias avoid places, environments, things, and even types of people, such as clowns, even if there is no danger or hazard. Phobias are not necessarily the result of trauma affecting the object concerned. They usually develop without any obvious explanation and unexpectedly. It can cause anxiety just to think of a phobia.

Separation Anxiety Disorder

Someone has a separation anxiety disorder when separated from a caregiver; they experience high rates of distress. This depression is so severe that it interferes with social interactions and functioning. Children and adolescents are the majority of people with the disorder. Nonetheless, there are some rare cases where it is produced by adults.

Illness Anxiety Disorder [Hypochondria, Health Anxiety Disorder]

Those with an illness anxiety disorder are unnecessarily worried about getting sick or seriously ill. We also assume that even after medical tests show fitness, mild feelings or minor symptoms are indicators of serious diseases. Interestingly, their fear of the disease can often make them feel ill physically.

Obsessive-Compulsive Disorder [OCD]

Is a disorder in which a person has uncontrollable repetitive thoughts [obsessions] and actions [compulsions] they feel the urge to over repeat? Instead of fear, some people with OCD experience a sense of shame or something wrong during their compulsions.

Anxiety, however, can be a crucial factor in OCD growth at times. For instance, someone with OCD may have intense anxiety that if they do not practice their compulsive behaviors such as flipping on and off a light switch, something bad will happen.

2.3 Post-Traumatic Stress Disorder [PTSD]

PTSD requires a prolonged period of extreme stress and reaction to fight or flight that happens regularly despite the lack of stressors. Stimuli, such as slamming a car door, may cause symptoms of PTSD. Sometimes after suffering a trauma such as sexual assault or almost losing their lives, people develop PTSD. Nevertheless, PTSD can also develop without any major trauma.

Adults must have multiple signs that reflect the effects of the disorder in order to be diagnosed with PTSD. Anxiety, too, is a common symptom.

Anxiety is the common factor although these conditions are not defined by all mental health professionals as different types of DSM-V anxiety disorders, anxiety is the common factor in them all. If you're searching for a doctor to diagnose or treat you with one or more of these anxiety disorders with DSM-V, try to discuss anxiety with other problems.

Post-traumatic stress disorder (PTSD) has a clear relationship with other mental health disorders, such as drug use and anxiety or mood disorders. Get the truth about the link between PTSD, an anxiety disorder itself, and everything from acute stress disorder to panic and obsessive-compulsive disorder.

In addition to PTSD, mental health disorders, known as anxiety disorders include acute stress disorder, social anxiety disorder, panic disorder, prevalent anxiety disorder, obsessive-compulsive disorder, and serious phobia.

It's been found that people with PTSD are at higher risk of all these conditions. The summary includes the levels among people with PTSD for these anxiety disorders.

PTSD and Panic Disorder People with PTSD experience panic attacks as people with PTSD are at higher risk of developing panic disorder. In fact, about 7% of men and 13% of women with PTSD also have the panic disorder — a rate that is much higher than in the general population.

2.4 The Differences Between Panic Disorder and PTSD

PTSD and Social Anxiety Disorder Threat the symptoms of PTSD that make a person feel different as if they are unable to relate or communicate with others. Additionally, many people with PTSD experience high levels of depression, embarrassment, remorse, and self-blame.

It is, therefore, not shocking that PTSD and social anxiety disorder also co-occur with each other. Fortunately, therapies for both PTSD and social anxiety disorder are very successful. Read more about the social anxiety disorder diagnosis, its connection with PTSD, and how to get treatment for both conditions.

The correlation between PTSD and social anxiety disorder PTSD and obsessive-compulsive disorder studies found that between 4% and 22% of people with PTSD also had an obsessive-compulsive disorder (OCD) diagnosis. However, individuals with OCD are also highly likely to have witnessed traumatic events.

Another survey, for example, showed that 54 percent of people with an OCD claim diagnosis had experienced at least another traumatic event in their lives. While these rates are high, they are not completely surprising.

PTSD can make the life of a person feel overwhelming and out of control. Initially, OCD-related behaviors can help make a person feel more controlled, healthy, and reduce anxiety. Eventually, however, these approaches backfire, which leads to more anxiety and depression.

The correlation between PTSD and OCD Acute Stress Disorder and the risk of developing PTSD Acute Stress Disorder and PTSD often go hand in hand with each other. This is because only one month after the occurrence of a traumatic event can a diagnosis of PTSD be given. However, shortly after a traumatic event, people are likely to develop PTSD-like symptoms.

Acute stress disorder describes the PTSD-like symptoms encountered shortly after a traumatic event.

Individuals with acute stress disorder were found to be at higher risk of developing PTSD eventually.

Post-traumatic stress disorder and generalized anxiety disorder (GAD) may occur simultaneously. This is not completely surprising given that PTSD itself is an anxiety disorder that can manifest from one person to the next in different ways.

As such, PTSD can lead to other disorders that each have their own set of diverse causes, characteristics, and symptoms.

Other common anxiety disorders may include pain disorder (PD), social anxiety disorder, obsessive-compulsive disorder (OCD), and specific phobia in addition to GAD.

2.5 Understanding Generalized Anxiety Disorder (GAD)

Generalized Anxiety Disorder (GAD) goes far beyond most people normal worrying and fretting. It is defined as the excessive concern about subjects or events that persist for a minimum of six months.

The anxiety is something that the person does not seem to be able to control with the object of concern that often changes from one thing to the next. The worrying eventually takes up with little relief, a lot of a person's day, and to the point where relationships and jobs are affected.

A person is diagnosed with GAD with at least three of the following physical or cognitive symptoms: • Edginess or restlessness • Quick exhaustion or fatigue • Impaired focus or feeling as if one's mind suddenly moves blank • Irritability, either internalized or externalized • Increased muscle aches or soreness • Difficulty sleeping or unsatisfactory sleep • Physical anxiety symptoms.

2.6 The Relationship between PTSD and GAD

Research suggests that at some point in their treatment, about one in six individuals with PTSD experience GAD. It also shows that in people with PSTD, the prevalence of GAD is as much as six times massive as in the general population.

Although the causes for their coexistence are not entirely clear, we know that a common feature of PTSD is a concern. Since emotional responses in people with PTSD are usually hyper-aroused, it is also possible to extend and exaggerate problems to the point where they can no longer be managed. Concern can even be used as a coping mechanism in some individuals.

It's not unusual to hear people with PSTD say they're distracted from the issues that are more disturbing to them by thinking about other activities or problems.

Worry can distance them from the thoughts and feelings they cannot confront. Another possible explanation is the shared roots of PTSD and GAD. Although trauma is PTSD's underlying cause, it may also be the catalyst leading to GAD.

Other anxiety disorders that coexist with PTSD like GAD, will coexist with PTSD, other anxiety disorders that share similar causes and overlap symptoms. • Panic disorder (PD) is felt in about 7% of people with PTSD. It is marked by regular and sudden bursts of panic and persistent fears about future attacks. PD occurs four times higher in people with PTSD than in the general population.

• In 28% of people with PTSD, social anxiety disorder exists and is characterized by intense fear and social interaction avoidance. Having PTSD can be the natural consequence of the disorder as both are characterized by feelings of isolation and "not fitting in".

• Certain phobia occurs in 31 percent of people with PTSD and is characterized by the fear of specific things (such as spiders, blood, or dogs) or situations (elevators, bridges, heights). Individuals with PTSD are seven times more likely than the general public to have a phobia.

• Obsessive-compulsive disorder has been less studied in relation to PTSD, but evidence suggests that people with PTSD may have OCD somewhere between four and 22 percent. Excessive obsessive and/or intrusive thoughts and repetitive behaviors or thoughts (compulsions) characterize OCD.

Chapter 3: Stress Management & its Techniques

In our lives, we all experience stress. Because the vast majority of health issues are triggered or affected by stress, recognizing how stress affects your body and practicing successful stress management strategies is important to make stress work for you rather than against you.

3.1 What's the Stress?

Stress is the response of your body to your life changes. Since life involves constant change (from moving places from home to work every morning to arranging to some changes in life, such as a loved one's marriage, divorce, or death), there is no escaping stress.1 This is why the goal should not be to remove all stress but to eliminate unnecessary stress and handle the rest effectively. Some people experience certain common causes of stress, but each person is different.

Causes of stress can come from many sources known as 'stressors'. Because our familiarity of what is considered "stressful" is generated by our individual interpretations of what we come across in life (based on our own combination of personality traits, available resources, and habitual patterns of thought), a situation can be viewed as "stressful" by one person and merely "challenging" by another.

Simply put, the stress cause of one person may not register to someone else as stressful. That said, some situations in most people tend to cause more stress and may increase the risk of burnout. For example, when we find ourselves in circumstances where we are faced with high demands; where we have little power and few choices; where we do not feel equipped; where we may be harshly judged by others; and where there are severe or uncertain repercussions for failure, we tend to get stressed.

Because of this, their careers, their relationships, their financial issues, health issues, and more mundane things like clutter or busy schedules are overwhelmed by many people. Learning to cope with these stressors will help to reduce the stress experience.1 Stress effects Much as each of us perceives stress. Differently, stress affects us all in ways that are special to us.

One person may encounter headaches, while another may find a common reaction to stomach upset, and a third person may experience any of a number of other symptoms. While we are all reacting to stress in our own ways, there is a long list of commonly experienced stress effects ranging from mild to life-threatening. Stress can have an impact on immunity, which can affect virtually all health areas. Stress can also affect mood in many ways.1 if you have physical symptoms that you think may be associated with stress, talk to your doctor and make sure you do what you can to protect your health. Symptoms that may be aggravated by stress are not "all in your head" and must be taken seriously.

The development of a stress management program is often part of an overall wellness strategy.

3.2 Effective Stress Management Techniques

Stress can be handled successfully in many ways. A combination of stress relievers that tackle stress physically and psychologically and help develop endurance and coping skills are usually the best stress management strategies.

Highly effective relievers of stress

- Use fast relievers of stress. In just a few minutes, certain stress relief methods will act to relax the stress response of the body. Such strategies provide a "quick fix" that, at the moment, can help you feel calmer, and this could help in a number of ways. If your stress response is not activated, you will take a more reflective and constructive approach to problems. Out of anger, you may be less likely to lash out at others that can keep your relationships healthier. You can also prevent chronic stress by nipping the stress response in the bud.

Fast stress relievers, such as breathing exercises, may not develop your immunity to potential stress or reduce the stressors you face, but they may help calm the physiology of the body once the stress response is activated. In the midst of a stressful situation, certain strategies are less easy to use. But if you consistently practice them, they will help you to better manage stress by being less sensitive to it and more able to quickly and easily reverse the stress response.

Long-term healthy habits, such as exercise or daily meditation, can help foster resistance to stressors if you make them an important part of your life.3 Communication skills and other lifestyle skills can help manage stressors and change how we feel from being "overwhelmed" to being "challenged" or even "stimulated." You may not be capable of removing stress from your life or even the biggest stressors entirely, but there are places where you can mitigate it and get it to a manageable level. Any stress you can reduce can minimize your overall load of stress. For example, leaving even one toxic relationship can help you deal with other stresses you experience more effectively because you may feel less overwhelmed.4 discovering a wide range of stress management techniques and then picking a mix that fits your needs can also be a key strategy for effective stress relief.

Questions Frequently Asked About Stress Is Stress Inevitably Health Harmful?

In reality, no. There are several different types of stress, ranging from eustress, which is a positive and exciting form of stress, to chronic stress, which is associated with many serious health issues and is the type of negative stress most frequently mentioned in the news.1 While we want to manage or eliminate the negative stress, we also want to maintain positive forms of stress in our lives to help us recover. But even "healthy" stress can contribute to unnecessary stress levels if we encounter too much stress in our lives, which can lead to feeling overwhelmed or activating your stress response for too long. That's why learning to relax your body and mind regularly and reduce unnecessary stress whenever possible is still important.

How can I tell if I'm stressed too much?

Stress affects us all in various ways, not all negative. (In addition, the tension of an exciting life can actually serve as a good motivator and keep things interesting.) But, when stress levels get too high, many people experience some stress symptoms. Headaches, irritability, and' fuzzy thinking,' for example, can all be signs that you are under too much stress.1 While not everyone under stress can experience these specific symptoms, many wills. If you find that you don't know how anxious you are until you're exhausted, it's important to learn how to recognize the subtle signs and actions of your body, almost like an external observer might. You should try this body scan exercise to see how the body reacts to stress (it helps you relax at the same time).

When I feel overwhelmed by tension, what can I do?

From time to time, we all feel overwhelmed; that's natural. Although removing occasions when things conspire and the stress response of the body is activated virtually impossible, there are ways you can reverse the reaction of your body to stress rapidly, buffer the harm to your wellbeing and keep your mind open, so you can cope more effectively with what's happening right now.

Is there a way of being less stressed?

Hopefully, you can remove some of the tension you're feeling right now and become more resilient in the face of adversity in the future by practicing a routine stress management strategy or two. There are several different things you can practice, from a morning walk to an evening newspaper practice to just making more time for friends. The trick is to seek anything that suits your personality and lifestyle, and sticking with it is simpler.

3.3 Tips for Stress Management

There are several factors to consider before discussing stress management techniques.

The following tips are tailored to assist individuals with a stress management program from The American Psychological Association

Comprehend the tension. How are you stressing? For everyone, it can be different. You can be better prepared and reach your stress management toolbox when needed by understanding what stress looks like for you.

Identify the sources of stress. What causes stress for you? Whether it's work, family, change, or any of the thousand other potential triggers.

We all handle stress differently, so it is essential to be aware of the signs of your weight. What are your alarm bells inside? Low tolerance, headaches, discomfort in the stomach, or a variation of the Stress Signs

Recognize your coping tactics. What is your relaxing go-to tactic? These can be habits that have been learned over the years and are sometimes not the right option. For example, by self-medicating with alcohol or over-eating, some people cope with stress.

Implement proper stress management techniques. It is good to be aware of any existing negative coping patterns so that you can turn them out for a healthy option. For instance, if you're going to over-eating, you might instead practice meditation, or decide to call a friend to talk through your situation. The American Psychological Association suggests that the most effective way to create positive change is to switch one behavior at a time.

Make self-care a priority we put our well-being before others when we make time for ourselves. But it's like the airplane analogy — we need to put on our oxygen mask before we can help anyone. The most natural aspects that facilitate well-being are often ignored, such as sufficient sleep, food, leisure, and exercise.

Self-care is the care of the community.

If you feel overwhelmed, contact a friend or family member with whom you can chat. Talking to a health care professional can also reduce stress and help us learn healthier coping strategies.

3.4 Various Approaches and Methods for Stress Management

These ideas are something that we can all gain from doing more. The plans are classified into three groups:

1. Action-oriented approaches: used to move to improve a stressful situation

2. Emotion-oriented approaches: used to alter our perception of a stressful situation

3. Acceptance-oriented approaches: you can't control when coping with stressful situations. Consider the strategies below and find out what combination works best to keep the stress levels under control.

Action-Focused Solutions Action-focused solutions encourage you to respond and improve the stressful situation.

As reported by Nelson & Harrell: "Stress is unavoidable, depression is not"

Be assertive, the secret to being confident is clear and compelling communication. We can question what we want or need when we're assertive, and also clarify what's troubling us. The trick, while still having empathy for others, is to do this reasonably and firmly. You will stand up for yourself until you understand what you need to do and be constructive about improving the stressful situation.

You can learn more here about how to be assertive.

Reduce noise, they can help slow down by shutting off all the equipment, screen time, and repetitive stimulation. How many times are you going offline? For your own sake, it's worth changing.

Make time every day for a little quietness. You may note how all those things that seem to be urgent that we need to do are becoming less critical and crisis-like. There will be that too - do list when you're in a place to come back to it. Recall that recharging is a very effective way to deal with stress.

If we let them, our days are going to overtake us. The months were fairly full before we knew it. We create a less stressful and more joyful life when we prioritize and arrange our activities.

With these tips, you will learn more about time management here.

Boundaries are the internal set of regulations that we set for ourselves. We outline what habits we are going to accept and will not embrace how much space and time we need from others, and what our goals are.

Chapter 4: Coping with Overthinking and Depression

Should you think you overthrow yourself all the time? Are the feelings so constant that you don't feel like your own subconscious is going to let you be? Continue to know read-and what this might be.

4.1 Disorder of Overthinking-What's it?

There is no over-thinking condition. There are different types of anxiety disorders that include a person in overthinking or ruminating, but there is no disorder. It can barge into your quality of life when a person cannot stop obsessing and worrying about things.

Several mental health problems where an individual cannot stop his or her brain from ruminating are PTSD, depression, agoraphobia, panic disorder, selective mutism, separation anxiety disorder, social anxiety disorder, phobias, substance-induced anxiety disorders, or it may be a symptom of some other disease.

Many of them overthink as a symptom when it comes to anxiety disorders. For example, when they're going to have a panic attack again, a person with panic disorder might ruminate and overthink. They are obsessed with something that might cause their assault. We are not only nervous but now they have meta-anxiety, which is fear about anxiety. A panic attack over-thinking made it feel more overwhelming.

It's normal to overthink. Just indulge in excessive rumination, you don't have to have an anxiety disorder. You may argue that this is part of the human condition. At times, we all overthink things: you may be overly concerned about what you have said or done to someone. At work or at school, you may be nervous about performing. You may be worried about how others see you. These are all examples of how to overthink yourself.

Some forms of overthinking include: — When you're concerned about what you should have said or done — performance anxiety, or worried about how you measure up to others at work — participating in "what - if" scenarios where you're wondering what might happen in a variety of circumstances — catastrophic or worst-case thinking — worrying about getting an unforeseen panic attack — excessive Most people suffer from intrusive problems that are beyond their control and stress about them. Cognitive Behavior Therapy (CBT) is a common treatment for this type of anxiety. CBT helps individuals challenge their negative or irrational thinking and turn their thoughts into positive, productive ones. Getting anxiety therapy or counseling can make a big difference to overthinking someone. You should work in your local area with a therapist or with one of Better Help's certified mental health professionals. Online counseling is a great place to work on anxiety and learn how to cope with it.

Overthinking Most people are familiar with the term anxiety disorder (and, in fact, every day millions of people are suffering from some type of anxiety disorder), but we tend to overlook a major anxiety disorder symptom that overthinks.

Ruminating or obsessing about something is the result of overthinking. Many people think that they are over thinkers when listening to this description. By overthinking something, who doesn't go a single day? We're wondering if we're making the right choices from small things like choosing the fastest route that morning on our commute or choosing the right restaurant for dinner to things like the well-being of our children and the safety and security of our families. That's usual, though. To some extent, it is normal in stress and overthinks.

Nevertheless, overthinking can have harmful effects on a person mentally and emotionally. It would be repetitive thoughts about something that triggers one anxiety, tension, fear, or dread while overthinking as it relates to an anxiety disorder. It's not just worrying too much about something - it's so obsessed about something that it affects your ability to work in your life.

When you're wondering or concerned about yourself, your job, your family, your friends, or anything else, and you don't have an overthinking problem, whatever you're thinking about, you're worried for a while, then you're moving on with your day after a short period of time. Sometimes you keep worrying, but you don't ruminate endlessly. The anxiety doesn't mess with the rest of your life. Nevertheless, with overthinking as a consequence of an anxiety disorder, the worry is all about which the individual may think, and although they may not obsess with the same thing all the time, they are always worried about something.

If you think you may suffer from anxiety overthinking, you may have found that you have experienced one or more of these situations:-Difficulty following and contributing to a conversation because you go over and over potential responses or statements until the conversation has either ended or the window of opportunity to speak has been Lost-Continuously comparing yourself. But all those who experience it will find that their quality of life is affected by their inability to control negative thoughts and emotions effectively. It can make it harder to go out and socialize, enjoy sports, or be productive at work because their mind spends excessive time and energy on different thinking lines. There is a sense of not having full control over their own minds or emotions, which can be dangerous to one's mental health.

It can be difficult to make friends or keep them overthinking because you are struggling to communicate when something is wrong, or you may talk overly. Speaking to them can be extremely hard because you're nervous about what to do or do with them because you're deeply concerned about how you're going to do or what's going to happen. Someone who overthinks may even struggle in a normal environment to carry on general conversations or interact. We may even have trouble going to the supermarket or an appointment.

The reality is that overthinking can have an impact on your life, anything, and everything. It can affect the way you communicate with others, it can affect your social life, and it can affect your personal life. What this means is that it can begin to wear away from you and your relationships with the people around you. Overthinking in your life will create serious problems.

4.2 How to Stop Overthinking

"Stop overthinking things!"

You've learned this many times, and it's not helpful at all. You can't just turn over a switch and stop thinking about it. In reality, being told to stop overthinking always ends up thinking more about issues. It is a loop of viciousness.

Essentially, not to overthink yourself is a long process you have to train your brain to do. Let's look at some common reasons for overthrowing and teaching how to avoid overthinking.

Insomnia Overthinking Your mind will race when you can't sleep, and you may have obsessive thoughts about getting to sleep. Also, when insomnia occurs, this overthinking happens, and then the next day begins. You can feel tired and less concentrated on your brain. You may have negative thoughts about not being able to sleep and obsessive thoughts.

For some reason, insomnia is considered a vicious cycle. It's hard to stop worrying about not sleeping when you've had it. Here are a few ways in which you can reduce sleeping problems.

• Applications for meditation and concentration. They allow you to live right now, discarding any intrusive thoughts or feelings that you may have. Apart from the fact that your brain can be educated in mindfulness, it can calm you down and make sleeping easier.

• When you can't fall asleep, get out of bed. If you're in bed and you can't sleep, it sounds like you can't get out of bed. The subconscious shares the restlessness of your brain. Get out and do relaxing activities. Don't spend time or do something relaxing on social media. On the opposite, relax.

• Make sure you won't die from lack of sleep. While you're threatened by your fear and anxiety that you can't sleep, most cases are acute. While your health rejects from chronic sleep deprivation, it will make the problem worse if you worry too much about an occasional bout of insomnia. It's best to see a doctor or therapist if the problem persists.

Decision making another reason people overthink is that they make decisions. Sometimes it's a big decision. Sometimes, there's something a bit stupid about the decision making, like what restaurant to choose.

While you should think about your decisions, it's time to overthrow them, especially if you've got a fair amount of people waiting for you to make the decision. Here's how to conquer the uncertainty of decision-making.

• Consider your decision-making time limits. Now, it doesn't have to be that short this time limit that you feel exhausted, but it should be small enough to help stop overthinking.

• Many people, especially the big decision-makers, schedule their time of thinking and end up being distracted in the meantime. Taking some downtime to think will keep anxiety from being overthrown.

• Again, it can help to be conscious and to live in this moment. The present moment will include the decision-making rationale, not the groundless concerns that you may have.

• You may change your mind on a decision in some cases. To know this can make a decision easier.

4.3 Overthinking and Anxiety

Many mental disorders can lead to overthinking, and there is an obvious connection between anxiety and overthinking. Those who are anxious never live in the present.

Parts of the brain are always concerned about what's going on next, and extreme anxiety and overthinking can make it difficult to leave home.

Here's how to interrupt and overthink fear when your nervous brain tells you no. Your nervous mind can overthink things by setting goals too high. Anxiety and overthinking make setting bigger goals challenging for you. You will work your way up by setting smaller goals.

- Again, the importance of meditation and mindfulness cannot be emphasized. Many mental illnesses are healthy, especially when it comes to anxiety and overthinking. Meditation can bring you back to the present moment and, if anxiety hits, relax your body.

- Discover what causes you to overthink your nervous brain. Triggers can make your mental illness worse, and it makes it easier to handle by spending time writing down what triggers your overthinking and anxiety.

- Distractions in anxiety and overthinking are always significant. Why you should actually begin to pay attention to your issues, distractions will help to reduce your anxiety, tension, and other problems. Try to watch a video or a jigsaw puzzle.

- Start noticing when you have an anxiety attack rumbling. Then, try to get out. Anxiety and overthinking, particularly if you know what the causes are, can often be avoided.

- It's time to see a doctor if your anxiety and overthinking is too much and takes up all your energy.

Overthinking and anxiety are two things that go hand in hand, but you can make things much better by controlling your anxiety and overthinking.

4.4 Bipolar Disorder and Overthinking

They tend to think about the mental health facts they care about when one speaks about bipolar disorder. And that knowledge about wellbeing is the reason that people with bipolar disorder appear to be either depressed or manic. Those with it have a difficult time controlling their mood, but with overthinking, they may also have a hard time.

In bipolar disorder, both sides of the coin will overthink disturbing or distressing thoughts. One may be worried about what will happen in the future with depression. And, they may be concerned about the drug's side effects.

With mania, you may find it difficult to pay attention to your thoughts, making it more difficult to challenge your thoughts. It is quite difficult to separate real life from fiction at times. And, maybe you're so euphoric that you spend time to feel protected and then regret it.

It is very important to seek the aid of online therapy or an in-person therapist for bipolar disorder. In mild to moderate cases, online therapy works extremely well. A psychiatrist can provide you with basic information about bipolar disorder and mental health statistics. Therefore, it is important for you to pay attention to your thoughts.

Your depressive symptoms can sometimes last for long periods of time, and your emotions can make them worse. You can focus on the negative and trigger long periods of time to exacerbate your condition. Our thoughts that pop into our minds, bipolar disorder or not, tend to make the problem worse. If you need assistance, seek help.

You might wonder how to stop thinking about positive thoughts. One way is to think about more positive thinking. At this, you should roll your eyes. You assume that, by definition, positive thoughts are something that comes straight from a cheesy health book.

Science, however, agrees that the key to success is positive thoughts and more positive thinking habits. There are some ways to do that if you want to think more positively.

- Take a look at your bias to confirm. Negative thoughts tend to linger, and it's usually the opposite when it comes to positive thoughts. You should try a little bit to improve your thought.

- Continue hearing your positive thoughts instead. Write it down as you start to think positively. Note that you think and collect positive thoughts.

- It is not something we can explain enough. Practice conscientiousness. This helps you to let go of some emotional distress. Through the window passes a negative image. Focus the positive thoughts on your mind.

- Recall all the times you helped people. Think of something you're content with. Some feelings of anxiety, just let them go. It is a series of steps that need practice.

- Many people believe that positive thinking does not mean negative thinking at all. Anything that worries, no matter how large it is, should be overlooked. That's not at all, really. Positive thinking simply means doing less negative thinking in the department of overthinking. It's going to happen distressing feelings, but positive thinking tells us that emotional distress is temporary and that there's a lot to think about.

- Try to clean your social media feed. Eliminate the ones that are more pessimistic and concentrate on positivity. Yeah, you should also absorb negative news, but many people are overwhelmed with it, and it's not good for you if you're an over thinker.

4.5 Mentally Strong People

It is less likely that mentally strong people would overthink. Think of the muscle of your brain. The more you train it, the better you will be mental. It is particularly important to increase your confidence in mental health as you age. Mental health declines with age, but you can train your mind with the right health information.

Here's some good information for your mind about mental health: • mentally strong people do a lot of exercises. You can imagine strong people strengthening your body when you think of exercise. Exercise, though, has a lot of positive side effects for your health. Your brain, for example, releases good chemicals that destroy pain and help lower your hormones of stress. Not to mention, exercise helps to distract you from your worries, making it great if you want to know how to stop worrying about it.

• People who are mentally healthy are able to socialize as much as possible. Try to talk to a close friend and go further to reach them. Seek to get out and chat with someone in a shop, cafe, or other location if you don't have any mates to talk to. As you talk to other people and try to make friends, you feel a lot less anxiety and more information.

• People with mental strength undergo cognitive behavioral therapy on a regular basis. A type of therapy helps you get rid of bad habits and feelings and can be used to treat mental illness of all types. Eating disorders, bipolar disorder, a widespread disorder of anxiety, and more.

• Strong people tend to be emotionally educated by putting it together. It can have some negative side effects to do the same things over and over. Look at any aspect of your life and think differently about what you can do. Try a new hobby, go for a dream job, or just learn something new. This helps with your overthinking when you start living for a new day.

- Strong people need to understand the moments of weakness will occur. There are moments when you're spending too much time thinking, and then you're overthinking. It's going to happen, so you can't overthink it. This happens at times. Don't just spend hours on it. You should arrange a period to let your mind wander over a particular issue and stop thinking about it when that time is up. This may take practice, but it can certainly be done by strong people.

You may wonder why there's "reduce tension" on here. Okay, it goes hand in hand with tension and our propensity to overthink. Stress is the way our body protects us when we are over our heads in a situation that challenges us, but our body is unable to tell the difference between real danger and normal tissues, and therefore the stress piles on.

People tend to find it difficult to cope with all of their pressures.

It can be nice to have some work. Positive psychology-related stress, which is healthy stress, helps to push you and make you want more. But it only goes so far with positive psychology. Too much stress can make your issues worse, including• Making you afraid of rejection, shame, disappointment, or losing everything.

- You appear to be worried about things that you can't change. Some people realize they should be thinking about the things they can change and forget the things they can't change, but that's hard to overthink.

- Physical stress is an unnecessary stress issue. This hurts every day, literally. Physical stress means that stress has consequences that are actually painful. Physical stress manifestations include headaches and other body aches, which can also be clinical depression.

Stress will occur to anybody. Whether you're a kid, a teen, or an adult, it doesn't matter. Here are some trouble-free ways to reduce stress if you have a pattern of overthinking and causing tension. Anyone can do these simple ways, nor do they need a doctor in these simple ways.

• Cognitive behavior therapy. This is something that takes practice, but it is important to learn to recognize thoughts that are by nature, distracting and to learn how to cope with these thoughts.

• Write down and order the issues from the most critical to the least. Part of solving problems involves first solving the easiest issue and moving upwards. Eventually, you will find it easy to solve problems.

• Remember the fear of failure and other every day worries. Why are you scared of that? How do you have an effect on your stress? Are you afraid of guilt, failure, or something else?

• The importance of working out is not understood by men. When quirking a little, it can help to reduce the tension.

• Take a little time to relax. See what's going on in your favorite series. Don't spend too much time relaxing, but rather take a break and come back with a fresh mind.

• Do not take alcohol or drugs. If they are prompted to prescribe medication by talking to a doctor or counselor, take it.

• At last, try to work with a counselor. They can help you with your problems.

4.6 Hypochondria

Hypochondria is another aspect of overthinking and common anxiety disorder in general. This is when you still believe that you have something wrong with them medically, making overthinking it a big problem.

Several individuals are slightly hypochondriac. You may anticipate something is wrong with you, for example, usually after seeing Dr. Google, so you're talking to your doctor. Instead, you find that nothing is wrong, and it's just an issue with overthinking, combined with a touch of common anxiety disorder.

You might be an extreme hypochondriac, though. You're still talking about something with your doctor today. You still have those feelings after you talk to your doctor, and there seems to be no discussion with your doctor to make them go away. You still think you're sick, no matter how much you try.

You need to seek help with this. You may have more than just a common condition of anxiety. You will finally work up the courage to say you're good after having counseling.

While many people are cynical about motivational speakers, they might be able to help. You can be encouraged to read stories about a man who has been able to overcome fear and survive or people who have learned to start living at an older age and is a good way to deflect you from overthinking.

It's a good way to get some personal level of mental health knowledge. Although some of this knowledge regarding mental health may not be part of current psychology, some should be checked out.

Spiritual psychologist and author Eckhart Tolle, for example, is a good place to go for information about health. "Eckhart Tolle, a spiritual psychologist, and author," you ask. Eckhart Tolle wrote a lot of books about the here and now, about which health information about avoiding overthinking tends to speak.

A psychologist, Guy Winch, is also a good listener. It is worth checking out any author of emotional advice.

Read all the health information you can get when it comes to an understanding. Most books are short, and it doesn't take much time to read them. Some take a lot of time, but it's worth the information they give. Some self-help books sound a little cheesy, but you're going to be shocked how much healing, rejection, remorse, disappointment, and other things can help.

It is important to ingest all the quality of mindfulness you can when it comes to overthinking. Mindfulness is the secret to getting the assistance you need.

Chapter 5: PTSD Coping Strategies

Nonetheless, getting PTSD can be a natural response to any number of distressing situations, such as sexual abuse, physical assault, injury, or any kind of violence. PTSD symptoms include increased anxiety— especially followed by frequent traumatic event flashbacks, sleeplessness, and avoidance of locations or social situations that might cause flashbacks. There are 7.7 million adults living with PTSD in the United States, and women are twice as likely to experience this disorder than men, according to America's Anxiety and Depression Association (ADAA).

Post-traumatic stress disorder may last for years, and its symptoms may affect the overall quality of life. That being the case, often simplistic approaches to deal with PTSD symptoms may be tempting. Pessimistic coping strategies on the spur of the moment may seem useful, but they can easily become self-destructive in the long run. These may include using alcohol or recreational drugs to relieve your feelings, decrease tension, or quiet your thoughts.

Alcohol and other drugs that start with the edge but may cause addiction when used as a substitute for proper care, such as cognitive-behavioral therapy (CBT) that has been accepted as a "safe and effective solution" to this condition. So what are the things you can do to keep your PTSD symptoms under control, apart from your doctor's prescribed CBT and any other medications?

5.1 Few Approaches to Consider

1. Increasingly, thoughtfulness-based meditation and relaxation techniques have been shown to help manage a range of disorders. A careful examination of PTSD medications points to a few therapies found to be effective in reducing isolation and self-blame in people diagnosed with the condition. Those are • Awareness-based stress reduction (MBSR), an intense 8-week program focused on the practice of awareness meditation that targets to train people to focus their attention on their breath and learn how to avoid being carried away by distracting thoughts • Awareness-based cognitive therapy (MBCT), described as "adaptation to MBSR," has a very equivalent structure but is designed to do so.

2. Most people who have been diagnosed with PTSD say that finding an enjoyable physical activity they can do on a regular basis has helped them reduce their stress levels and deal with their symptoms.

Rebecca Thorne, who after childhood trauma was diagnosed with PTSD, describes how running helped her deal with the symptoms that had an impact on her life.

"I am a driver," she says, "and I am suffering from [PTSD]." "One of the many things I'm thinking about while I'm running, and also when I'm not, is the relationship between the two." "I enjoy running in all-weather [...], always with a considerable amount of climbing. When I battle my way up the climbs, I always believe that the hill is my disease, and I'm going to conquer it slowly and steadily.

The sport allows veterans, according to the team, to reach a concentrated mind state known as "flow," in which they are so immersed in the game that all other thoughts and feelings are pushed aside.

Dr. Nick Caddick, who has been involved in the study, compares this to the impact of meditation on consciousness, just because it is more intensive. Medical News Today also reported on a study that suggested that Tai chi — a form of martial arts — can help war veterans relieve their symptoms of PTSD.

3. Aromatherapy Another study reported by MNT earlier this year showed that essential orange oil could be effective in reducing symptoms of PTSD-related chronic stress and anxiety. This study was conducted only in mice, however, and these findings are still to be replicated in a cohort of people. Share on Pinterest some says that in handling chronic stress aromatherapy can be beneficial. Nonetheless, some people diagnosed with PTSD have said that aromatherapy can be a good tool for relaxation and is effective in reducing stress levels.

Sezin Koehler — who has been treating her own PTSD symptoms for many years — writes, "Lavender, ginger, peppermint, or any other therapeutic oil massaged on the spot between your eyebrows, and your pulse points are beautifully calming." Writer and retired Thames Valley Police Officer David Kinchin, who was diagnosed with PTSD in the 1990s, also recommends the soothing effect of aromatherapy in one of h.

"Aromatherapy can form part of a therapeutic regime as well as be a preventive treatment in its own right. It provides pleasure through the sense of touch (massage), the sense of smell (aromatic oils), the sense of sight (pleasant surroundings) [...] by doing so, it helps to create favorable conditions in body and mind for healing to take place very naturally."

4. Art Therapy

Art therapy is a form of PTSD therapy that has been picking up steam in recent years.

A type of therapy, conducted by professionals trained to work with people who have experienced traumatic situations, aims to help individuals outsource their feelings and learn to cope with distressing memories through art, such as painting or sculpture.

One case study illustrates how art therapy can help people diagnosed with PTSD and traumatic brain injury to overcome their symptoms and continue using art projects creatively to leave behind their distressing experiences. Research researcher Melissa Walker, who serves as an art therapist, explained in a dedicated TED talk why and how art therapy could be effective in treating PTSD. Walker helps the individuals she works with to create masks and examine the impact on their lives and personalities of the traumatic experiences.

"Whoever has undergone trauma has a barrier that prevents them from verbalizing what they have experienced," she says in an interview. "There is a pause in the (convolution of) Broca, the part of the brain responsible for language and speech. The mask gives them a way to elaborate themselves. The visual picture of the mask unleashes words. It reintegrates into the left and right hemispheres. Now they can discuss their thoughts with their social worker or psychiatrist." Melissa Walker 5. Pets for PTSD Another method that is apparently effective in helping people cope with PTSD's debilitating symptoms is the introduction of a pet that is specially trained to understand and prevent — or interrupt— such symptoms from arising.

A bunch of studies have shown that having a trained animal has a positive impact in helping people overcome depression and anxiety linked to PTSD, as well as other symptoms such as hallucinations, at least in the short term. Last year's research indicated that spending as little as one week with a specially trained dog improved symptoms of PTSD by 82 percent.

Richard Steinberg, a veteran who has been diagnosed with PTSD, says his dog "can feel when [he] has a nightmare, night sweats," and she becomes restless, doing her best to catch his attention, "trying to get him out of the situation." 'Putting my hands on her calms me down and calms her down" he adds. "She feels the chemical changes in my body." Post-traumatic stress disorder (PTSD) people also deal with regular and severe anxiety symptoms. These strong anxiety symptoms often lead people with PTSD to rely on unhealthy coping methods such as drug or alcohol consumption. Fortunately, there are variety of safe ways to cope with the anxiety that can help reduce anxiety, become less severe and/or more tolerable.

Deep respiration can be effective in learning coping ability. It may sound stupid, but it does not breathe properly in many people. The diaphragm, a large muscle in your abdomen, is involved in normal breathing. You will stretch your belly as you breathe in. Your stomach will collapse as you breathe out. With time, people forget how to breathe and use their chest and shoulders instead. It results in quick and shallow breaths, which may increase stress and anxiety.

Fortunately, "re-learning" how to relax is not too late to help protect yourself from stress. To improve your breathing and fight anxiety, practice this simple exercise.

5.2 The Use of Relaxation Exercises

The use of relaxation exercises can be an effective way to reduce your stress and anxiety. One relaxation technique called progressive relaxation of the muscle focuses on a person alternating throughout the body between tensing and relaxing different muscle groups. This method of relaxation resembles a pendulum. You can achieve full muscle relaxation by first going to the other extreme (i.e., by tensing the muscles). Therefore, by tensing the muscles (a common anxiety symptom) and immediately relaxing them, the muscle tension symptom may become a sign of relaxation over time. In this article, you can learn basic exercise in progressive muscle relaxation.

Mindfulness

It can be very helpful to be conscious of anxiety. Since years, carefulness has been around. Nevertheless, experts in mental health are beginning to recognize that knowledge can have many benefits for people with problems such as anxiety and depression. In a nutshell, it's about being in contact with the present moment and being mindful of it. We are lost in our minds so often in our lives, caught up in the fear and worries of everyday life. This exercise will introduce you to your awareness, and it may be helpful to get you out of your mind and in touch with the moment.

Self-monitoring

Self-monitoring can be a helpful way to manage the symptoms of anxiety. We are all "habit animals." Sometimes, without thought, we go about our day, missing much that is going on around us. In some cases, this may be helpful, but other times, this lack of awareness can make us feel like our thoughts and emotions are totally unpredictable and unmanageable. We can't really cope with anxiety's unpleasant effects without first being aware of what circumstances these emotions bring up. Self-monitoring is an easy way to raise awareness of this.

Social support

It has been found over and over again that helping people resolve the negative effects of a traumatic event and PTSD can be a major factor in finding support from others. Finding someone you trust can be very helpful when going through stressful situations or when validating emotionally. Only having someone at your side to speak to may not be enough, though. A supportive relationship has several important pieces that can be especially beneficial in helping someone overcome their anxiety.

Self-Soothing

It is important to have ways to cope with those feelings when you experience anxiety. Checking for social support, for example, can be a great way to improve your mood. However, sometimes the anxiety associated with PTSD symptoms can occur unexpectedly, and social support may not be readily available. Hence, learning coping strategies that you can do on your own is important. Often coping strategies aimed at improving your mood and reducing the anxiety you can do on your own are described as self-care or self-care coping strategies.

Using journals to deal with and communicate your thoughts and feelings (also known as descriptive writing) can be a good way to deal with anxiety. In order to improve physical and psychological wellbeing, creative writing has been discovered. In fact, creative writing has been shown to have a number of benefits, including increased coping and post-traumatic development (or the ability to find meaning in and have positive life changes after a traumatic event), as well as decreased symptoms of PTSD, anxiety, and frustration.

Diversion, in addition, the purposeful use of distraction techniques can be helpful in dealing with intense and stressful emotions such as fear and anxiety. Distraction is all you do to take away your mind from strong emotions momentarily. Sometimes it may feel much worse and more out of reach when concentrating on strong emotion. Therefore, you should allow the emotion some time to decrease in intensity by temporarily distracting yourself, making it easier to control.

Anxiety and avoidance of behavioral stimulation go hand in hand. Although avoiding anxiety-provoking situations can help to reduce our anxiety at the moment, it can prevent us from living a productive and rewarding life in the long term (especially as this avoidance is becoming larger and larger). Behavioral simulation is a great way to increase the level of activity as well as the amount of constructive and rewarding behaviors you partake in. You will reduce your depression and anxiety by triggering your actions.

Chapter 6: Dealing with Trauma

6.1 Trauma Defined

The longer we're alive, the more likely we're going to experience trauma. Trauma is the reaction to a profoundly distressing or traumatic occurrence that overwhelms the capacity of a person to deal with it, triggers feelings of helplessness, diminishes their sense of self, and capability to feel the full range of experiences and emotions.

It doesn't discriminate, and it's popular worldwide. World health organization (WHO) found that trauma had been experienced by at least one-third of the more than 125,000 people surveyed in 26 countries. That number increased to 70% when the category was restricted to people with core conditions as described by the DSM-IV (the classification used in the Mental Disorders Diagnostic and Statistical Manual, 4th edition). But those numbers are only recorded for instances; the real number is likely to be much, much higher.

While there is no objective standard for determining which incidents may cause symptoms of post-trauma, situations typically involve loss of control, deception, abuse of power, impotence, pain, frustration, and/or loss. The incident does not need to escalate to war, natural disaster, or personal attack in order to deeply affect an individual and transform their perceptions. Traumatic conditions that cause symptoms of post-trauma vary dramatically from individual to individual. Nevertheless, it is very subjective, and it is important to bear in mind that its reaction determines it more than its cause. Ultimately, trauma can be described as a psychological, emotional response to an event or experience that is deeply distressing or upsetting. This definition of trauma may apply to something traumatic when applied loosely, such as being involved in an accident, developing a disease or injury, losing a loved one, or going through a divorce. It may also include the far extreme, however, and include encounters that are seriously harmful, such as rape or torture.

Due to the subjective view of events, this broad definition of trauma is more of a guideline. Everybody views a traumatic event differently as we face them all in our lives through the prism of previous experiences. For example, one person may be angry and scared after going through a storm, but somebody else may have lost family during Hurricane Katrina and barely escaped from a flooded house. A moderate Category One hurricane will bring up traumatic flashbacks from their terrifying experience in this situation.

Psychologists have established definitions as a way to differentiate between forms of trauma because trauma responses spread across a wide spectrum. These include complex trauma, post-traumatic stress disorder (PTSD), and traumatic developmental disorder.

Complex trauma occurs over and over again. It often contributes to the victim being directly harmed. Complex trauma symptoms are cumulative. The traumatic experience often happens within a specific timeframe or relationship, and often in a specific setting. Post-Traumatic Stress Disorder (PTSD) may grow after a person has been subjected to or confronted with a traumatic incident. The sufferers of this PTSD have their ordeal's constant and debilitating thoughts and memories.

Developmental Trauma Disorder in the field of psychology is a new concept. During the first three years of the life of a child, this disease develops. Developmental trauma, arising from violence, neglect and/or abandonment, interferes with the physical, cognitive, and psychological development of the baby or child. It interferes with the willingness of the victim to connect to an adult caregiver. An adult who infects developmental distress does not generally do so deliberately–instead, it occurs because they are unaware of children's social and emotional needs.

6.2 Trauma Symptoms

A typical reaction to a traumatic event is often shock and denial. Such emotional reactions may fade over time, but a survivor may also experience long-term reactions. These may include frustration Persistent feelings of sadness and anxiety Flashbacks Unpredictable Emotions Physical symptoms such as nausea and headaches, Intense feelings of guilt as if they are somehow responsible for the incident an altered sense of shame Feelings of isolation and hopelessness Trauma therapy is not one-size-fits-all. To address different symptoms, it must be adapted. Specially trained mental health professionals will evaluate the unique needs of the patient and prepare care specifically for them.

6.3 Modalities for Trauma

There are currently several modalities for trauma therapy in place: Cognitive Behavioral Therapy (CBT) helps the client to become more aware of their stressful thoughts and beliefs and gives them skills to help them respond to emotional triggers in a healthy manner. Exposure therapy (also known as in Vivo Exposure Therapy) is a form of cognitive-behavioral therapy used to reduce the anxiety associated with the trauma-related emotional triggers.

Talk therapy (psychodynamic psychotherapy) is a verbal communication technique used to help a person find relief from emotional pain and reinforce the constructive forms the patient already possesses of problem management. Both modalities address the memory part of the trauma (the unconscious), but we now know that the conscious brain of a victim still needs to be treated. Recent studies have found that body-oriented approaches, including meditation, yoga, and EMDR, are important tools to help reconnect mind and body. In addition, neuro feedback (a form of biofeedback based on brain waves) shows promise to help patients with PTSD symptoms learn to change their brain wave behavior and help them become calmer and more capable of communicating with others.

Healing from Damage Emotional and psychological trauma can be healed. They recognize that the brain changes in reaction to a traumatic experience, but you can put the trauma behind and learn to feel safe again by collaborating with trauma-specific mental health professionals. You may have been traumatized, if you have witnessed an extremely stressful or upsetting incident that makes you feel helpless and out of control emotionally. Psychological trauma can leave you dealing with feelings, memories, and anxiety that will not go away. You may also feel numb, detached, and unable to trust others. It may take a while to conquer the pain and feel safe again when bad things happen. But you can improve your healing with these self-help techniques and assistance. Whether the trauma happened years ago, or yesterday, you will make changes in recovery and move forward with your life.

6.4 What is Emotional and Psychological Trauma?

Emotional and psychological trauma is the product of extraordinarily traumatic events that make you feel helpless in a menacing world. Traumatic experiences often involve an ultimatum to life or health, but any circumstance that leaves you feeling overwhelmed and helpless, even if it does not involve physical damage, can lead to trauma. The assessment of whether an incident is traumatic is not the objective circumstances, but the subjective emotional experience of the event. The more you feel scared and powerless, the more likely you will be traumatized.

Emotional and psychological trauma may be caused by • One-time events such as an accident, injury, or violent attack, particularly if it occurred during childhood or was unexpected.

• Chronic, constant stress such as living in a crime-ridden community, battling a life-threatening illness, or regularly witnessing traumatic events such as bullying, domestic violence, or childhood neglect.

• Commonly overlooked triggers such as surgery (particularly in the first three years of life), the sudden death of someone near, the break-up of a significant relationship, or a humiliating or deeply disappointing encounter, especially if someone was deliberately cruel.

Facing a natural or manmade disaster trauma can pose unique challenges — even if you weren't directly involved in the incident. In fact, while it is highly unlikely that any of us will ever be the direct victims of, for example, a terrorist attack, plane crash, or mass shooting, we are all constantly bombarded with horrific images on social media and news sources from those people who have been. Over and overseeing these images will confuse your nervous system and create stress.

Childhood trauma and risk of future trauma:

While traumatic incidents can occur to anyone, you are more likely to be traumatized by an occurrence if you are already under heavy stress, have experienced a series of losses recently, or have been previously traumatized — especially if the earlier trauma has occurred in your childhood. Childhood trauma can result from anything that distorts a child's sense of security, including

- an unhealthy or dangerous climate

- Parent separation

- Serious disease

- Intrusive medical procedures

- Physical, physical or verbal abuse

- Domestic violence

- Neglect Experiencing childhood trauma can result in severe and long-lasting effects.

If trauma to childhood is not overcome, a sense of fear and helplessness progresses to adulthood, setting the stage for further trauma. Nonetheless, even if the trauma happened many years ago, you can take steps to heal the pain, learn to trust and reconnect with others, and restore your sense of emotional equilibrium.

Psychological trauma symptoms we all respond to trauma in a variety of ways, experiencing a wide range of physical and emotional reactions. There is no 'right' or 'wrong' way of thinking, feeling, or reacting, so do not judge you're own or other people's reactions. Your responses to ABNORMAL events are NORMAL reactions.

Emotional and psychological symptoms:

- Surprise, confusion or doubt
- Confusion, concentrating problems
- Rage, irritability, mood swings
- Anxiety and anxiety
- Guilt, guilt, self-blame
- detachment from others
- Feeling depressed or helpless
- Feeling detached or Physical numb symptoms:
- Insomnia or hallucinations
- Fatigue
- Concentrating difficulties
- Rapid pulse
- Engineering.

But even if you feel better, you may be distracted by painful memories or feelings from time to time — especially in reaction to stimuli such as an incident anniversary or something that reminds you of the trauma. You can develop Post-Traumatic Stress Disorder (PTSD) if your psychological trauma symptoms do not ease — or if they get even worse — and you find that you are unable to move on from the incident for an extended period of time. While emotional trauma is a normal reply to a traumatic incident, when the nervous system is "stuck," and you stay in psychological shock, unable to understand what happened or manage your feelings, it becomes PTSD.

6.5 Trauma Recovery Tips

Whether or not a traumatic event causes death, you must cope with the loss of your sense of security, at least temporarily, as a survivor. The natural response to the loss is grief. You need to go through a mourning process like people who have lost a loved one. The mentioned tips will help you cope with grief, recover from the pain, and move forward with your life.

Trauma recovery tip 1:

Having trauma going disrupts the natural balance of your body, trapping you in a state of hyper arousal and terror. In addition to burning off adrenaline and releasing endorphins, exercise and movement will help to rebuild the nervous system. Try to practice most days for 30 minutes or more. Or if it's faster, it's as nice as three 10-minute spurts of exercise per day. A rhythmic exercise that works best for both your arms and legs— like walking, cycling, swimming, basketball, or even dancing.

Add an element of knowledge. Instead of concentrating on your emotions or distracting yourself while exercising, focus your attention on your body and how it feels when you walk. Notice, for example, the feeling of your feet hitting the ground, or your breathing rhythm, or the feeling of wind on your skin. Rock climbing, wrestling, weight training, or martial arts will make it easier— after all, during these exercises, you need to focus on your body movements to avoid injury.

Tip 2: Don't isolate

You may want to withdraw from others after a trauma, but solitude just makes things worse. Connecting face to face with others will help you heal, so make an effort to keep your relationships going and stop spending too much time alone. You don't need to explain the pain. There is no need to think about the pain and communicate with others. That can actually make things worse for some people. Comfort comes from someone else's feeling engaged and embraced.

Ask for help. While you don't have to talk about the trauma itself, it's important to have someone with you to express your feelings face to face, someone who listens carefully without judging you. Turn to a trusted member of the family, relative, lawyer, or cleric. Participate in social activities, even though you don't like it. Do with other people "natural" activities, activities that have nothing to do with the traumatic experience.

Get back to old friends. If you have withdrawn from relationships that once mattered to you, seek to reconnect. Join a support group for survivors of trauma. Connecting with others with the same challenges will help to reduce your sense of isolation and hear how others can help inspire you to heal.

Volunteer. Volunteering can be a great way, as well as helping others, to counter the sense of helplessness that often follows trauma. Mind your strengths and helping others regain their sense of power. Build new mates. It is important to reach out and make new friends if you live alone or far from family and friends. Take a class or join a society to meet like-minded people, connect with an alumni association, or reach out to neighbors or co-workers.

Often people who have had trauma ==feel disconnected, withdrawn, and find it hard to communicate with others==. If that fits you, you should take some steps before you meet a friend next: exercise or transfer. March up and down, swing your arms and legs, or just walk around. Your head will feel clearer, and the connection will be easier for you. You are toning the voices. Vocal toning is a great way of opening up to the social engagement as strange as it sounds. Sit up straight and just make sounds like "mmmm." Adjust the pitch and volume until a nice feeling is felt in your ears.

Tip 3: Self-regulate your nervous system

No matter how irritated, anxious, or out of control you feel, it's important to know you can adjust and relax your arousal system. It will not only help to ease the anxiety associated with trauma, but it will also give rise to a greater sense of control.

Aware of breathing. Practicing mindful breathing is a quick way to calm yourself if you feel disoriented, confused, or upset. Just take 60 breaths and concentrate on each' out' breath. The input of the sensory. Does a particular sight, smell, or taste make you feel calm quickly? Or perhaps petting an animal, perhaps listening to music helps to soothe you quickly? Everybody responds a little differently to the sensory input, so experiment with different methods of rapid stress relief to find out what works best for you.

To stay grounded. To feel more rooted in the moment, sit on a chair. Feel your feet against the chair on the ground and back. Look around and pick-six items in them that are red or blue. Note how deeper and calmer the breathing is.

When you feel it, let yourself feel what you feel. Recognize and acknowledge your thoughts about the trauma as they emerge. The Emotional Intelligence Toolkit from Help Guide can help.

Tip 4: It's important to take care of your health:

Having a healthy body will improve your ability to cope with traumatic stress.

Get a lot of sleep.

After a traumatic experience, the sleep patterns may be disrupted by anxiety or fear. But deficiency of quality sleep can exacerbate your symptoms of trauma and make your emotional balance more difficult to maintain. Go to sleep and get up every day at the same time, striving for 7 to 9 hours of nightly sleep. Remove drugs and alcohol. Having them will aggravate the symptoms of trauma and increase feelings of depression, anxiety, and loneliness.

Eat a healthy diet.

During the day, eating small, well-balanced meals will help you keep up your energy and reduce mood swings. Avoid fried and sugary foods and eat plenty of omega-3 fats — such as salmon, walnuts, soybeans, and linseeds — to boost your mood. Lower heat. Try relaxation techniques like meditation, yoga, or exercises of deep breathing — schedule time for things such as your favorite hobbies that will bring you joy.

It's easy to take.

Try to slow down things and turn down the pressure to perform at the top of your game — and try to resist criticism when things aren't ideal. It's all right to have a Netflix binge for one weekend, but you don't want to turn self-care into social isolation.

If your mind spins about what this awful event means about the planet, the future, etc., remember to eat balanced, nutritious meals and snacks, "one step at a time." We may want starchy or sugary comfort foods such as macaroni and cheese or chocolate cupcakes during periods of stress. It's okay to indulge in something, but don't make it a routine. High-fat and high-sugar foods in the brain activate the same reward centers as drugs such as cocaine. This makes you feel better at the moment, but like heroin, it doesn't help anything in the long term.

Go out. Go out.

Go on a stroll and get some sunshine. A deficiency of vitamin D can feel like a depressive episode, so it might make you feel a little better to soak up the antidepressant of nature — sunlight.

Practice.

Whether it is gentle or hard, it will lift your mood to get your body moving.

Hear your body.

If this week, you're tired of getting more rest earlier than usual. Emotional distress is taking its toll and may need to heal the body.

Do something that's social.

It can be good to be around other people, especially loved ones. And it can create other issues to isolate yourself. If you think it would be good for you to socialize, make some plans for low stress.

Consider discussing your thoughts.

Some people like to talk about what they thought, but if you don't want to talk about it too, it's okay. Journaling could be a good way to release emotionally.

Return to the track.

Return as soon as possible to your daily routines. This helps with the structure and operation. But with loved ones, carve out special time too.

If you are living the life you dream to lead, think about it. Things like these make for a perfect time to re-evaluate our goals and think about whether what we do in life really matters or whether it makes us happy or value our talents.

Many people can overcome the effects of a traumatic event and, after a couple of weeks, feel like themselves again. But if you still feel sad, or use drugs or drink more than before, please contact your primary health care provider or a cognitive behavior therapy consultant or therapist.

6.6 Healthy Ways to Cope with a Crisis

What are some healthy ways to get through to the other side and deal with a crisis? Here are some tips that should be kept in mind when facing a crisis. Focus on what's Important It is important to focus your time on dealing with the aftermath of a crisis. Simply getting through the day is attainment, so it should be important to shut down your obligations to just do that. Order take-out so you can cut back on shopping and cooking, put unnecessary commitments on hold, and only focus on what requires to be done to keep your physical and emotional energy intact.

Find Support, Support If others are aware of your trauma, and they're likely to offer help, now's the time to take it on. Let your loved ones lighten your burden by assisting with tasks or a supportive ear. Later, when you're up to it, you can repay the favor, and they need something. By receiving support, you can feel better, and others are likely to feel better by being able to do something to help. That's the best thing friends do.

Lessen Your Stress Response When you are experiencing a crisis (or even when someone near you is experiencing a crisis), the stress response of your body may get triggered and stay triggered, keeping you in a state of permanent stress. While feeling "relaxed" in the midst or after a crisis may be difficult, you can practice stress relief techniques that can reduce the potency of your stress levels, help you to reverse your stress response, and feel more resilient to what's next. Process Your Feelings Whether you're writing in your newspaper, talking to a good friend, or consulting a therapist, putting words into your experience to better integrate it is important.

As you move through the crisis, for fear that you will' wallow' too much and get' stuck,' you may be tempted to ignore your feelings, but processing your feelings will allow you to move through them. Make sure you eat a healthy diet, get enough sleep, exercise regularly, and do other things to keep the body working at its best to avoid adding to your problems. Seek to do some things you normally enjoy, such as watching a movie, reading a good book, or gardening to alleviate some of the tension you are feeling.

Sometimes people who are dealing with a calamity or trauma wonder if their negative reactions are a sign of weakness, or if they are dealing with things the' right' way. While there are increasingly healthy ways of dealing with troubling situations, be patient with your feelings and reactions to things. After major or even mild trauma, it's natural to feel' not yourself,' and acknowledging yourself and your emotions can help you feel better and make things easier to handle.

If you experience invasive thoughts and feelings, have recurrent nightmares, or are unable to move through your life the way you need due to your reaction to the trauma, even after few days, you may want to talk to a professional about your affairs to make sure you get the Support you need.

Even if you don't have any major problems but just feel like talking to someone might be a good idea, it's better to err on the side of getting extra help. Taking care of yourself is a smart and responsible way.

Chapter 7: Ways to Deal with Volatility and Anger

7.1 Understanding Anger: Explosive, Passive, Chronic

What really is Anger?

You know how it feels.

The person in front of you drives ten below the speed limit when you're running late. When your machine starts to fail in the middle of a busy working day, and you unexpectedly feel the urge to throw it through the air.

Anger is characterized as a motivational condition correlated with violence by the National Institute of Mental Health (NIMH). Like other emotions, indignation triggers biological responses such as rapid heart rate, elevated adrenaline, and increased levels of hormones. Anger can be originating by both internal and external events, according to the American Psychological Association (APA), indicating that you may be upset with an individual, a situation, a personal problem, or a past incident. Even trivial things can cause intense rage that is hard to control for people who struggle to control Anger.

Simply put, rage is a powerful emotion— and either we're learning to control it, or we're letting it rule us. But not all rage is equally generated. Passive Anger what's important about Anger is that it doesn't always feel like rage. Anger is almost completely undetected in one of its most dangerous and strong ways. It's buried deep inside where it transforms into something that feels like rage almost nothing— this is known as passive frustration.

Since passive Anger can be much more difficult to recognize, understanding the signs is crucial.

7.2 5 Passive Rage Identification Methods

1. Studies into fear and anxiety show that Anger repressed transforms into anxiety. When a person is deeply hurt and the resulting rage is never properly addressed, unhealthy coping mechanisms may be formed to prevent the same type of hurt from occurring again. One will have to become hyper-vigilant in this process — always scanning for potential threats in one's climate. This creates fertile ground for the development of an anxiety disorder.

2. Repressed Anger in isolation can ultimately drive a person away from a healthy community. This is because rage contributes to other people's distrust. A person with repressed Anger will most likely feel insecure in situations that he/she is unable to manage. As a result, these individuals tend to exhibit unpredictable social behavior — for example, involving society and then withdrawing unexpectedly at random.

3. The repressed rage of apathy often contributes to hopelessness — or an attitude of "sky is falling." Hurt, suffering, and loss anxiety can effectively prevent a person from living honestly. There may be a lack of motivation or emotional energy to do the things that he / she most wants. Over time, this type of behavior may lead a person to see themselves in the world as fatally flawed or useless. Passive Anger may eventually turn into a debilitating depression if left unaddressed.

4. Health problems 85% of all diseases can be related to our emotional state, according to the Conservative Center for Disease Control (CDC). Certainly, there is no lack of data to show that

negative emotions — and particularly Anger — can wreak havoc on the whole nervous system. Passive Anger's long-term physical effects include headaches, digestive disorders, insomnia, anxiety, depression, high blood pressure, autoimmune diseases, heart disease, and stroke.

5. Relationship Trouble Repressed rage can cause a person to long for intimacy, but at the same time, greatly fear it. Many who suffer from childhood abuse or neglect are unable to trust in adulthood close friends or romantic partners. If the hurt and subsequent frustration felt has never been addressed properly, friends and romantic partners can later become stand-ins for the hurtful agent. Until the rage is understood, there are likely to be dysfunctional relationship trends.

Have you ever noticed someone who cut you off in traffic, blaring your car horn a little too long? It's okay. All of us were there. These kinds of moments are a small taste of explosive rage — the most widely recognized kind of Anger, perhaps. It's an unexpected and volatile type that often comes as a surprise — not just to those around you but to yourself as well.

While explosive rage is most frequently found in males with issues with substance abuse, most people experience at least some of it in their lives. A prolonged type of explosive rage, however, leads to dangerous behavior in some individuals, including verbal outbursts, physical violence, property damage, and emotional abuse. When intense frustration continues, one of the following anger-related mental health disorders could be a symptom

7.3 Anger-Related Mental Disorders

1. Intermittent Explosive Disorder, those with repeated outbursts of explosive rage, may have what is known as the Intermittent Explosive Disorder (IED), a condition that affects an estimated 16 million Americans. IED is a mental disorder characterized by episodes of unwarranted and destructive rage.

According to the NIMH, a person must have had three episodes of impulsive aggressiveness out of proportion to any associated psychosocial stressor in order to be diagnosed with IED. Anxiety, depression, or alcohol, and drug abuse can also affect individuals with this condition. When you, or someone you know, suffer from what might be an IED, they are strongly encouraged to seek professional assistance from a licensed counselor.

2. Disruptive mood dysregulation disorder (DMDD) is the most common mental condition found in children according to the NIMH. Extreme irritability, rage, and regular, extreme outbursts of temperature define it. DMDD signs include almost constant irritable or angry mood, extreme physical or verbal outbursts, at least three times a week, and deteriorating and disruptive short-tempered moods. Nevertheless, signs must be present for at least 12 months in order for a child to be diagnosed with this condition.

3. Borderline Personality Disorder;

Borderline Personality Disorder (BPD) is a mental illness characterized by moods and actions that are highly dysfunctional. It is hard for individuals with BPD to control feelings, exhibit impulsive and reckless behavior, and have extremely unstable relationships with others. The NIMH stated that individuals with this condition typically experience co-occurring conditions such as depression, an anxiety disorder, self-harm behavior, and may even demonstrate suicidal philosophy and behavior.

According to NIMH, BPD signs include:

• Extreme emotional responses to the possibility of rejection, whether real or perceived • A history of dysfunctional relationships with others, ranging from strong closeness to extreme dislike or frustration

• Unstable self-image and low self-esteem

• Impulsive and risky behaviors

• Frequent suicidal thoughts and behaviors

• Deep, persistent feelings of depression.

Although BPD may be difficult to diagnose, therapy has been shown to be effective in reducing this disorder's debilitating effects. Individuals with BPD symptoms continue to see the best results when treated by combining psychotherapy and medication.

7.4 Chronic Anger

Do you know someone who, from the instant they wake up to the time they go to bed, seems irritated? He or she may have persistent rage. Individuals with chronic anger are said to have a tenacious and pervasive frustration of life, others, and themselves, and may seem to be in a constant quest for their rage outlets. Such people may also suffer from an attitude of the victim— believing that their situations are beyond their control, and often others are working against them deliberately.

In other words, it is always something for those with chronic frustration. And until these individuals seek help in changing the negative patterns of thinking that drive their chronic anger, they are likely to experience difficulties in the workplace, relationships, and overall health. Because of the prolonged nature of this form of anger, "Anger Management 101" individuals are at a higher risk of developing associated health issues such as high blood pressure, heart disease, and autoimmune diseases. Chronic rage has also been associated with mental disorders, including depression, anxiety, and other mood disorders.

But we are not here to give a bad rap to anger. Have you ever felt the pounding of your adrenaline when you saw someone wrong? Even at the risk of facing painful or unpleasant consequences for your actions, did you stand up for someone else?

Not everyone's rage is a bad thing. There is definitely a need for healthy frustration. We're wired for a cause with the power to get mad. Healthy wrath is more constructive than destructive. This motivates us to overcome fear, fight for the right thing, and bring about positive change in the world — even if that often means only standing up for ourselves or others. The aim is to ensure that we know how to handle our rage safely. So how are we going to turn our anger from destructive to constructive?

7.5 Useful Things to Try

Deal with your History

Most people hesitate to deal with past wounds, particularly those that happened in childhood, because they are afraid to linger in the past or develop a mindset of the victim. But in the past, coping with the past does not linger. In reality, you can really move past them only by discussing the difficult things you've encountered. Find a reliable mentor or try a psychologist who can help you get through the work and recover from the issues that fuel the continuing frustration.

Open the door.

It is important to preserve mental health and develop a sense of connection with trusted individuals. Invest in a people's culture with which you can be open and honest. Clearly voicing your worries and concerns to people you trust will help you gain perspective, gain insight, and learn new ways of maintaining control of your emotions.

Save from festering.

Will you find yourself reviving events and remembering something else you'd have said or done? Are you getting angry again about something that really doesn't matter? Such kinds of habits of thinking establish a breeding ground for developing anger problems. Not only do these negative thinking habits contribute to outbursts of anger, but over time they can also cause crippling anxiety and depression.

Take one (or two) breather.

Although it may take practice, before reacting to someone in frustration, you may learn to handle a situation completely. You can find that the situation does not warrant the anger-infused response you originally imagined offering when you give yourself time to cool off. Through allowing we time to process, we may see that our present circumstances are not as threatening as they seemed at the moment (or involve the level of anger).

Get the rest of your skin.

Skipping out on sleep is a very effective way to become irritable. Just cutting corners — an hour here and an hour there — can have a tremendous impact on the chemical balance that helps us to maintain a healthy outlook, minimize our emotional responses, and maintain self-control. It's worth coming home from a night out early or waiting for your favorite show to catch up on the weekend. Consider sleep a priority, and you will gain more control over your feelings quickly — anger and others.

Eat the greens all over.

For some, a simple dietary change can alleviate considerable stress due to chemical imbalances in the body. If you snack on highly processed foods on a regular basis or grab fast food dinners on the run, this could contribute to your bad moods. Consider talking to a licensed nutritionist about your symptoms and collaborating on a healthy food plan that will help you achieve a healthier biochemical balance.

Use the weights to level it out.

Exercise is a very powerful way to release frustration and pent up rage. It not only allows you to maintain a healthy chemical balance (hello endorphins!), it also increases self-confidence and relieves stress. Try a yoga class or jog around your neighborhood if weightlifting isn't your thing (try for 10,000 steps a day, which is 5 miles and places you squarely in the "healthy" category). No matter what type of exercise you take, you may quickly find that you have a more positive outlook on life if you commit to sweating it out for at least 30 minutes a day.

Hit the library.

Only learning how to handle rage is one of the most powerful ways to gain control of your life. This article is certainly a good start, but keep learning about the signs and symptoms of toxic rage and researching the stories of others who have managed to resolve it. Comprehension of the thought-patterns and emotions involved is half the battle when it comes to mental health. If you can't get it to a library, countless online resources (ahem, Thriveworks.com) are available. Pour a little coffee and dive in.

At first, it's never easy to gain control of your thoughts. It takes time and effort, and it's a perfect way to practice mindfulness. Pray, meditate, do yoga, go for a walk and enjoy the beauty that surrounds you, or just find a quiet place to focus on the "inner feelings" about yourself and others that you have not yet noticed. Try to get out of your own mind for a while after that — let your emotions wash over you without making any judgments about it. You can gain more control over your thoughts and emotions by learning to be present at the moment.

Anger is a natural and normal human sensation that tends to make its existence known in any relationship, even if the person to whom it is expressed is not addressed. Sadly, in our relationships with those we love most, including our romantic partners, rage still raises its head. Yet passion in a relationship should not mean uncontrollably voicing emotions like rage. Controlling frustration and controlling your reaction to an angry partner is a valuable skill in any romantic relationship that can foster intimacy and maturity.

As a therapist, I also encourage my clients to think about how the way they want to be a partner gets their reactivity in a relationship. We shut down so often, complain to friends, or try to control our partner as a reaction to our frustration. While we may feel relieved at the moment by these tactics, they are rarely effective in the long run. Let's look at four easy approaches in your relationship to handle frustration and increasing maturity.

When a person struggles with their significant others, they may sometimes feel the urge to slam a door and give them the silent treatment. Going silent may temporarily calm you down, but it is likely to increase the anxiety or anger of your partner. This does not mean that in the heat of the moment, you have to sit down and solve a problem. Consider telling your partner that you need some time to calm down so you can organize your thinking instead of zooming out of the driveway or walking away. Let them know that you need to work out the difference and consider what a reasonable amount of time it takes for you to think and come back to them.

If your partner, having forgotten an anniversary or skipped dinner with their parents, tends to give you the silent treatment, you've probably experienced some anxiety that doesn't know what's going to happen. You can't get them to talk to you, but you can share that when they're ready, you're willing to share your thoughts and work together. Trying to force them into a rapid reconciliation or threaten them is likely to backfire and cause them to cut even more.

7.6 Focus on Managing Yourself

When we are upset with someone we love, we always feel compelled to please and soothe them as quickly as possible. Yet we can't ultimately monitor the feelings, actions, or emotions of anyone — we're just responsible for managing our own. Being calm is much more useful than trying to comfort someone else, and people who can stay focused on controlling their own emotions and reactions give space to do the same to the other person. So instead of asking, "Calm down, please! "Try slowing down your heart rate and taking a few deep breaths.

Similarly, if you are angry with your partner and want them to change their behavior, your attempt to control them will likely produce an adverse reaction. The aim is to share your thoughts with the expectation that the other person will be understood, not to shame. Note, if your words and actions activate the fear response in the brain of your friend, it is unlikely that you will be noticed. Throughout relationships, immaturity begets immaturity so often. Sending a rude text to your spouse while they're at work or waking those up with your complaints in the middle of the night may be important, but these tactics seldom do more than exacerbate a dispute.

Be mindful of triangles it can feel cathartic to complain to a relative, your kids, or even your therapist when you're angry or peeved at a partner. This is often called a relational triangle when we use a third person to control our uncertainty about another. It's completely human to want to wind up, and it's not wrong. But this "triangle" also prevents us from figuring out the issue in the original relationship, and it can make the partner feel alone or even more defensive. And when you're angry with your spouse next time, and you're tempted to pick up the phone, ask yourself, "Do I ask for help or just look for someone to agree with me? "If it's the latter, perhaps try to calm down before you ask someone else to do that. And while there's nothing wrong with sharing relationship tension with your therapist, be mindful that being impartial so helping you do your best thinking is their job— not agreeing with you that your partner is the story's villain.

For individuals, there are certain subjects that are likely to spark off an angry reaction or a nervous reaction that can lead to conflict. These are often issues such as finance, politics, faith, gender, parenting, or family drama. It is easy to assume that having different opinions will cause frustration and conflict, but our adolescent responses to these issues are more common than our actual opinions. Therefore, rather than relying on conflict resolution as quickly as possible, shift your focus back to responding as maturely as you can. This doesn't mean you have to deal with a partner's violence or volatility or even remain in a relationship. Maturity just seems to be determined not to let the feelings run the show absolutely. It seems to say, "What is the best version I do in this situation? "So your best self-slamming doors or screaming at people you love are unlikely to be seen.

Remember that you are 50 percent of the equation if you feel overwhelmed by the amount of anger in your romantic relationship. If you're calmer and mature, your relationship will be more calm and mature. Either your partner will grow to the same maturity level, or maybe you will know the partnership isn't right for you. You choose not to let rage run the show anyway. When one person can make a choice for himself, they will probably find a partner who can do the same.

Anger Style: Explosive what it looks like: "If you once again leave your jacket on the floor, I'll leave you! "Pushing you over the edge can take a lot, but when you get there, the world shakes, and people are running for cover. Why you might do it: If you've never been taught how to handle frustration, you might swallow it until you can't swallow it anymore. Your roof will eventually blow. Some people are angry junkies who get off on an emotional explosion's adrenaline rush, not to mention the fact that the attack can mean they're getting their way — at least in the short run.

The damage: It's virtually impossible to feel empathy and frustration simultaneously, so you're more likely to say and do overly rasp things that you later regret in the heat of the moment. Wait for it. How to turn it around. "Research has shown that the reaction to cognitive rage lasts less than two seconds," says Ronald Potter-Efron, Ph.D., anger management professional at Eau Claire, Wisconsin, and Letting Go of Rage's co-author. Beyond that, remaining angry requires a commitment. Recite the Pledge of Allegiance mentally or count to 10 and see whether the desire to scream has decreased. Own your emotions. Rephrasing your emotions clearly will help you feel more in control. "Your behavior really upsets me" is much more successful and efficient.

7.7 Anger Styles and Coping Strategies:

Anger Style: Self-abuse what it looks like: "He doesn't help me, it's my fault? I'm a terrible wife. "Each time you find a way to make all your fault. Why you might do it: your self-esteem took a beating somewhere along the way, and you realized that being mad at yourself is sometimes safer and easier than being mad at someone else. The damage: you can set up constantly turning angry feelings inward for continued disappointments and even depression.

How to turn it around• Ask yourself a question. If you feel the urge to blame, start by asking yourself, "Who told me that I was responsible for that? "Then ask,' do I really think so? "Thank you for recognizing the trend in the first place, instead of taking all the blame.

Focus on self-esteem. Make a list of your good qualities. Developing a true sense of dignity is a critical step in resolving self-indulgence. If you need more guidance working on this issue, seek out a specialist. Anger Style: Evite what it feels like: "I'm all right? It's all right. Everything's perfect. "Even when your intestine is burning with a fireball of anger, you put on a happy face and dodge every frustration show. This is not passive aggression; aggression is buried.

Why you might do it: "Women, in particular, are advised to be polite no matter what, over and over again. Get angry, and you might lose your credibility, family, friends, or work, "Potter-Efron says. You might not accept that rage can be controlled or conveyed peacefully if you grew up in a violent or abusive household. The damage: Anger's primary function is to show that something is wrong and to promote resolution. You may end up engaging in self-destructive behaviors (over-consuming, unnecessary shopping) by missing the warning sign. Ultimately, you can give the green light to the bad behavior of other people or refuse them the opportunity to make corrections. How can they apologize if they don't know that you were hurt?

Challenge your core beliefs• How to turn it around. Tell yourself, "Is it really nice that my workers leave early whenever they want? To go to golf every weekend with my partner? "If you're honest, you probably have a resounding answer to these questions," you know what? Recognizing that something is wrong is the first step in fixing it. Get out of sight. Imagine being hurt, overworked, or ignored by a friend. What's the right way for her to respond? Make a list of acts she might take, then ask why she's okay, but not you, to behave like that.

Adopt a successful conflict. Were you ticked off by somebody? In a supportive, constructive way, tell the person. Sure, he or she may be shocked by your words, perhaps even (gasp!) angered. And what are you thinking of? He or she is going to get over it. "Friends and partnerships are often more impaired by isolation than any expression of anger," Potter-Efron says. Anger Style: Sarcasm what does it look like: "You're late, it's OK. I've had time to read the menu — 40 times. "You've found a roundabout way to get your digs in, with a half-smile.

Why you could do it: you've been raised to believe that openly voicing negative emotions is not OK, so you're taking a more indirect route. It's their problem if folks get upset, not yours. You were joking, after all. Can't people take a joke? The damage: your cutting remarks will damage your relationships even if they are couched in wit. While some people insist that a mockery is a form of intellectual humor, the very word sarcasm has to do with the Greek phrase sarkazein, meaning "to break flesh like dogs."

How to turn it around • directly give it to them. "Sarcasm is a conversation that is passive-aggressive," says Todd. Find words to express your head-on thoughts. You could clarify to a late friend, assume, after you're sitting down, "I wish you'd try to be on time, especially if you know we've limited time." This is particularly true for children, to whom a gentle "Jumping on the furniture is not appropriate" sends a much brighter message than the snarky "Don't worry; we're only setting aside $2,000 for a new sofa." Once you hit your breaking point, cultivating assertiveness will help prevent a sarcastic streak from bursting out.

Anger Style: Passive-Aggressive Looks like: "Oops. Since I deleted all the old DVR baseball games? "You're not suppressing or swallowing your rage, but in an underhanded way, you're voicing it. You don't like conflict, but you're not a pushover either. "When people believe they can't stand up to others, they are' heart sneaks,'" says Potter-Efron. Many people, who by definition, are a conservative shift to this style when they feel forced out of their comfort zones.

Todd puts it another way: 'You're living your life around making sure other people don't get what they're looking for, rather than striving for what's going to make you happy.'

How to turn it around

• Authorize yourself to get mad. Say the rage is the way your mind says you're sick of being pushed around. A mantra:

assertiveness is subtle; there is no violence (passive or otherwise).

- Involve yourself. Instead of "forgetting" to hand in your report at work or show up late to meetings, gather your nerve and tell your boss that your workload has become too intense or that you have an issue with a colleague. It won't be easy, but it doesn't look for another job either.

Take supervision. When you resort to passive aggression when you are unhappy with what is expected of you, it is necessary to do something to take your situation's reins. Can't manage the house or the finances individually? Instead of doing a haphazard job (of course subconsciously), tell your partner how important it is to participate.

Anger Style: Habitual Irritation:

"I'm sick of borrowing my stapler from you! Choose some of your own! "This is often less of an incident reaction and more of an option by nature. It's always on if you don't turn it off consciously.

Why you might do it: If your anger dwells directly below the surface and continually flows through, disappointment, remorse, or dissatisfaction is likely to boil underneath. Perhaps the promotion was offered to your coworker, and you didn't. Maybe your wedding is going to fall apart, and you're not sure why.

The damage:

If you're always ready to blow, family, friends and colleagues may be taking great pains to avoid getting upset. Or they can altogether prevent you. The outcome that is most likely? You remain stuck in the same vicious cycle, no development.

How to turn it around•, getting into its heart. Who are you anxious about? When you dig deep, you'll realize it's probably not about a stapler, or dirty socks on the floor, or an empty carton of milk in the refrigerator, or anything else that makes you so upset. When you can't get to the bottom of it on your own, seek professional intervention.

• Change the indexes of indignation. Be aware of your irritation-related actions and feelings. Should you ball your hands into fists when you're angry? The pace in the room? Smiling, cursing, or grinding your teeth? As each physiological reaction is established and felt, make a deliberate attempt to do something — anything — otherwise.

• Imagine harmony. Use this method, before it overtakes you, to stop raising frustration. Picture a wind, a burst of light, or even a breeze in your breath. Watch it come in and out; every breath will be sincere and quiet in the best possible way. Hear yourself talking to yourself and others respectfully and quietly. Each time you do this photo, your rage reflex will diminish another degree.

Chapter 8: Forgetting Past Trauma and Anxiety

Most of them have at least one traumatic memory in their minds. One that still resonates for me was when my mother left me alone at the age of six to take home the babysitter. He told me not to be nervous because I felt apprehensive. "I'm going to be back there," she said, smiling brightly, driving away. As it became dark, I became more and more fearful that something had happened to her and that she did not return. I was completely scared by the time she came back. She heard me wailing outside. She scolded me and took me in. Years later, I would get worried and anxious when my wife came home late. My heart and mind will start to pound, and I had a full-blown panic attack more than once when she was especially late. I don't know I'm alone. Some have memories of a car accident, a murder, a natural disaster, a violent aunt, and a drunk friend, a stay in the hospital, an attack, and war horrors. Experiences such as these are more common than you might think, with an estimated 60% or more of Americans witnessing at least one of these at some point in their lives. Not all of these experiences cause people to experience pain later in life, but they can cause many problems and can weaken them for some. Persons with post-traumatic stress (PTSD) may become hypersensitive, with high-alert permanent nerves. Without warning, fear and anxiety recur, and nightmares may ruin sleep.

8.1 Memories and Trauma

But now there are simple but effective ways to easily remove the painful feelings that often surround these memories so that they can finally rest. Many people are able to do this work alone. Meeting with a therapist who is skilled in treating trauma can be helpful for more complicated traumatic memories.

Neuropsychologist Rick Hanson says in his book Hardwiring Happiness: The New Brain Science of Contentment, Stability, and Confidence, "Your brain was built in such a way as it developed, it was prepared to learn from bad experiences easily, but not so much from the good ones." That's why traumatic memories so often remain in our minds, while positive memories seem to slip away. "For the negative, it's an ancient survival mechanism that converted the brain into Velcro, but for the positive, Teflon," concludes Hanson.

Fortunately, new findings from affective neuroscience can help people recover traumatic memories that can lead to PTSD, depression, bipolar, and even Alzheimer's. One of the things we learn about memories is critically important: although the brain is especially good at storing bad memories, as we once believed, they are not permanently locked into the memory banks of the brain. This transforms and becomes susceptible to change once we consciously remember a memory.

Once we remember a memory, it becomes a little unreliable, and it can be changed for a period of maybe one or two hours before it rests in the brain again, or "reconsolidates." That's why, paradoxically, it can help us heal from old wounds by remembering bad memories. Reliving traumatic moments in a security situation will help a person to remove the memory from the intrusive "alarm" processes that cause so much discomfort.

In the book, The Archeology of Mind: Neuroevolutionary History of Human Emotions, Jaak Panksepp and Lucy Biven claim, "Emotional memories remain forever malleable, subject to manipulation by future events— through a phenomenon called reconsolidation." This is the foundation of numerous therapeutic strategies for healing trauma, including prolonged exposure therapy, supportive psychotherapy, and emotional liberation software.

8.2 How to Heal

Based on the latest research in neuroscience, Rick Hanson provides a simple yet effective strategy for redirecting the brain from the negative emotions associated with trauma to health and wellness-related positive emotions. Within his book, using the acronym HEAL, he outlines a four-step process.

Have a good experience.

Step 1 activates a positive mental state, installing it in your brain steps 2, 3, and 4. In step 1, we note a positive experience in the foreground or context of your perception that is already present. In the example I gave at the outset, I relaxed into an environment where I felt safe and encouraged and called to mind safety and security experiences.

Enrich it.

All too often, we spend minutes ruminating over a negative experience, and sometimes hours and days, but we gloss over the positive. We're taking the time to deepen the positive experience here. I'd open myself to my life's feelings of support. I'd imagine my wife and friends and the many benefits I have, filling my inner consciousness with a good memory of at least 10 to 20 seconds.

Absorb.

Here in the moment, we picture ourselves drinking. I imagine the feeling filled with all my cells. I feel it slipping into myself and being part of my brain and part of my whole being.

Link the content that is positive and negative.

Hanson argues that this is an optional move. We don't want the negative to overtake us, but to keep the negative in consciousness while the positive is absorbed. Hanson uses a garden's image. We imagine the beauty we're planting beautiful flowers. We become aware of the weeds and pull them out gently so that there is room for growth. He ends by saying, "Let go of all negative content whenever you want and just rest in the positive. Instead, in order to continue to eliminate the negative content, be mindful of only neutral or positive items that might have been correlated with the negative a few times over the next hour.

8.3 Forgetting Past

I bought back my mother's memories and some of the related feelings of becoming depressed when someone I cared about was late. By concentrating on the negative and triggering positive experiences, the traumatic emotions of the past will potentially be "erased." I can remember my mother leaving me alone and upset with me when she came back, but it doesn't seize me and shake me up as it uses and I'm much less worried when my wife comes home late. Everyone has memories that they'd rather forget, and they might know the causes that make them bounce back. Bad memories, from post-traumatic stress disorder to phobias, can underlie a number of problems. It is a natural human response to want to blot it out when an unwelcome recollection intrudes the mind. A hundred years ago, Freud suggested that people have a tool they can use to shut out of consciousness unwanted memories. Scientists have recently begun to understand how this works. Studies of neuroimaging have shown which brain structures play a part in intentional forgetting, and studies have shown that memories from memory can be intentionally blocked by people.

How are memories shaped?

- Sharing memories of Pinterest some can lead to fears and phobias.
- Proteins encourage the brain cells to grow and form new links for the mind of a person to store a memory.
- The stronger these neural associations are, the more we focus on memory or rehearse the specific events surrounding the memory.
- The memory remains there from time to time as long as we remember it.
- The older the mind, the more set it is, people thought for a long time, but this is not necessarily true.
- It becomes versatile again every time we revisit a memory. The relations seem to be malevolent and then reset. Each time we remember it, the memory will change a little, and it resets with every recall more intensely and more vividly.
- It's not even safe for long-term memories.
- This reinforcement process is called reconsolidation. Reconsolidation can slightly change our memories for better or worse. It can do the same to exploit this cycle.
- If something scares us when we're young, the recollection of that incident might become a little more terrifying every time we remember it, leading to anxiety that might be out of proportion to the actual event.
- A small spider that once scared us may grow bigger over time in our minds. There may be a phobia.

By comparison, throwing a positive light on an embarrassing memory, by turning it into a funny story, for example, may mean that it loses its humiliating power over time. A social gaff can turn into a piece of the group.

Why are so vivid bad memories?

Most people find bad experiences more than good ones stand out in memory. We break into our consciousness if we don't want them to. Scientists have shown that bad memories are more vivid than good ones, likely because of the connection between emotions and memories. This is particularly so when there are negative emotions and memories.

Neuroimaging has shown scientists that the encoding and recovery process includes the parts of the brain that process emotions, especially the amygdala and the orbitofrontal cortex. The greater the memory-related feelings, the more information we can recall, it seems. Studies of fMRI show increased cellular activity in these regions when someone has a bad experience.

Replacing memories Post on memories from Pinterest Unwanted will lead to anxiety.

For the first time in 2012, scientists at Cambridge University demonstrated which brain processes are involved in removing and destroying memories. We found that by using a part of the brain, known as the dorsolateral prefrontal cortex, a person can suppress a memory or push it out of consciousness to prevent activity in the hippocampus. The hippocampus plays a vital role in the memory of events. People may shift their consciousness to an alternate memory in order to replace memory.

Through two areas called the caudal prefrontal cortex and the prefrontal mid-ventrolateral cortex, they can do this. These areas are important in the presence of distracting memories to bring specific memories into the conscious mind. Suppressing a memory means shutting down parts of the brain involved in recalling. To remove a memory, those same regions need to consciously redirect the path of memory to a more desirable objective.

Dr. Michael Anderson, one of the authors of the report, uses this to either slap on a car's brakes or steer to avoid a threat. Functional magnetic resonance imaging (fMRI) was used by researchers to observe participants ' brain activity during an activity.

Such task included studying connections between pairs of words, and then attempting to erase memories by either remembering or suppressing alternative ones. Results showed that both techniques are equally effective, but that they activate specific neural circuits.

During post-traumatic stress disorder (PTSD), intrusive thoughts that keep on intruding into consciousness are plagued by people who have acquaintance with a traumatic life event. Understanding more about how to restore or block a memory might help people with this deteriorating disorder.

Changing contexts, the mental context in which an individual perceives an event affects how the mind organizes the event's memories. We remember events related to other events, where they took place, and so on. It, in effect, influences what causes such later memories, or how they can be recalled. Context can be anything connected to a memory. It could include meaning-related signs such as smell or taste, external environment, activities, feelings or thoughts around the time of the incident, incidental features of the object, for instance, where it appears on a list, etc.

Scientists have suggested that any process that changes our perception of that context may increase or decrease our ability to retrieve specific memories as we use contextual clues to recall information about past events. To check this, participants are set up by a team of researchers to memorize sets of terms when viewing pictures of nature, such as beaches or forests. The photographs were aimed at creating meaningful memories.

Until researching the second, some participants were told to forget the words on the first list. When the time came to remember the words, fewer words could be recalled by the party that had been told to forget. More interestingly, fMRI tracking also showed fewer image thoughts. They had lost the context in which they had memorized them by intentionally trying to forget the words. However, the greater the distance from the background, the fewer words they recalled. It means we should intentionally forget about it.

The researchers then told the audience to remember the words that didn't "wash" the scenes out of their minds, and they proceeded to remember the words and think about the pictures. The results may be useful to help people either remember things while learning, for example, or reduce intrusive memories while treating PTSD, for example.

8.4 Weakening Memories that Cause Phobia

Those with phobias are treated with access to the object that causes fear. Exposure therapy aims at developing the dreaded item's "free" memory that overshadows the old memory. The anxiety also returns over time while this works momentarily.

Researchers at the University of Uppsala and the Karolinska Institute in Sweden demonstrated in August 2016 that disturbing a memory can reduce its power. People who were afraid of spiders were windswept in three sessions in their experiment to pictures of their eight-legged friends. The objective was to disturb the memory by disturbing it and then reset it. First, by presenting a mini-exposure to spider images, the research team activated the fear of the participants. The participants then viewed the pictures for longer 10 minutes later. They saw the photos again the next day. By the third view, the researchers found that the brain portion known as the amygdala had less activity.

This represented in the participants a lower level of emotional involvement and a lower propensity to fear spiders. The scientists concluded that memory was unreliable from the first exposure. The memory was re-saved in a puny form when the longer exposure occurred. I say this keeps the anxiety from coming back too quickly. The researchers believe that in situations where exposure alone does not provide a long-term solution, this could improve strategies for dealing with anxiety and phobias.

8.5 A Drug to be Forgotten?

Share on Pinterest some medications, by removing bad memories, show potential to treat or avoid PTSD. Several scientists have proposed using medications to remove bad memories or the fear-inducing factor associated with them to supplement cognitive approaches. D-cycloserine is an antibiotic that also enhances glutamate production, an "excitatory" neurotransmitter that stimulates brain cells.

For one test, D-cycloserine was taken before a virtual reality exposure therapy by people with a fear of heights. Their stress levels were lower than before one week, and again three months later. In other studies, when, for example, a group of people with PTSD took propranolol just after recounting a bad experience while consolidating a memory, the next time the memory was triggered, they had fewer stress symptoms. Propranolol blocks norepinephrine, a chemical that plays a vital role in the mechanism of "fight or flight" and causes symptoms of stress.

New York researchers performed experiments on rats that showed it was possible to remove single brain memories by injecting a drug called U0126 while leaving the rest of the brain intact. Scientists used a drug known as an HDACi in a mouse study published in Nature in 2014 to remove epigenetic markers in the DNA that allow bad memories to live on. For example, this might help people with PTSD. Nonetheless, more research is needed on how to safely and effectively use these medications.

Memory manipulation going a step further, memory experts, including Julia Shaw, author of "The Memory Illusion," have worked out how to create false memories.

She starts by telling someone that they committed a crime when they were young, then adding layers of details until the person is no longer able to decipher reality from imagination. Shaw claims she does this to illustrate the misuse of some forms of questioning. Ethical issues not without ethical concerns are such methods.

Healthy people could use it to delete from the mind an unpleasant occurrence. Crime suspects may give people drugs that suppress memory to make them forget about events. Some bad memories, after all, serve a purpose. This will stop people from making the same mistakes again, or they can direct their actions in the future at certain times. How much should we forget?

Chapter 9: Relaxation Techniques

Relaxation for many of us involves tuning out at the end of the day in front of the Television or grabbing an extra sleep on the weekend. It does little to help reduce the adverse effects of stress on the mind and body, sadly. To combat stress effectively, we need to enable the natural response to relaxing the body. This can be attained by using relaxation techniques such as deep breathing, dreaming, reflection, and yoga, or by doing rhythmic movements such as biking, swimming, or walking with caution. Seeking ways to fit these things into your life will help reduce stress's negative impact and boost your mood and strength. We will also help you stay calm in the face of enemies and the unforeseen events of life. Stress is important for life's relief answer. You need imagination, thinking, and your very life to be stressful. Stress becomes dangerous only when it is debilitating and affects the healthy balance that your nervous system requires to keep in control. By generating the relaxing reaction, a condition of intense calmness that is the polar opposite of the stress response, relaxation techniques may throw the nervous system out of control. If your nervous system is overcome with pain, your body is filled with chemicals that brace you for "fight or flight." While in cases where you need to act quickly, the stress response can be influential, it wears down the body when triggered continuously. The reaction to relaxation puts the brakes on this heightened preparation condition and gets the body and mind back into a state of harmony. Generating the answer to relaxation a variety of different relaxation techniques can help bring the nervous system back into balance by generating the response to relaxation. The solution to relaxation is not to lay on the sofa or sleep, but a mentally productive cycle that leaves the body comfortable, peaceful, and concentrated. It's not difficult to learn the fundamentals of these relaxation techniques, but it takes practice. Many experts recommend that you set aside for your relaxing exercise at least 20 minutes a day. If that seems like a demanding undertaking, note that you can integrate many of these strategies into your current daily schedule (e.g., during lunch break at your desk). Knowing the most suitable relaxation technique for you there is no one relaxation technique that is perfect for all. Remember you're specific needs, interests, fitness level, and how you tend to react to stress while selecting a relaxation technique. The best approach for relaxation is the one that resonates with you, suits your personality, and is able to focus your attention and disrupt your daily thinking to evoke the answer to relaxation. You will find that mixing or merging different techniques in many situations can keep you focused and give you the best performance. Part of DHRM Staff Welfare how do you react to stress? Stress Response Signs Appropriate calming methods Over-excited frustrated, irritated, or keyed-up strategies that calm you down, such as yoga, deep breathing, or directed visualization Excited stressed, withdrawn, or staggered techniques that activate and energize the nervous system, such as rhythmic movement Frozen You continue to freeze: intensify in some respects when slowing down. If you are searching for peace, methods of solo relaxation such as yoga or gradual muscle relaxation can allow you the opportunity to quiet your mind and recharge your batteries. A community environment will give you the motivation and help you are searching for if you want social interaction. It can also help you stay inspired when training with others.

9.1 Relaxation Technique 1

Stress relief breathing meditation focusing on absolute, clear breaths, deep breathing is a simple yet powerful strategy of relaxation. Learning is easy, can be practiced nearly anywhere, and provides a quick way to check your stress levels. Deep breathing is also the foundation of many other calming techniques and can be paired with other stimulating components, including music. All you really need is to hang out for a few minutes and a spot. The trick to deep breathing is to breathe deeply from the belly and get as much fresh air in your lungs as possible. Instead of drawing shallow breaths from the upper chest, you inhale more blood from the belly. The more air you receive, the less stressed, the less breathless, and the more nervous you become. Sit up straight with your back comfortably. Place your chest with one hand and your stomach with the other. Inhale through the ears. The hand will grow on your chest. The hand is supposed to move very little on the stomach. Exhale through your mouth while squeezing your abdominal muscles, forcing out as much oxygen as you can. The hand on your stomach is supposed to move in as you exhale, but very little will shift the other hand on the shoulder. Keep breathing in and out through your mouth through your nose. Aim to inhale enough to push up and down the lower abdomen. List as you exhale gradually from 1 to 4. When you find it hard to breathe when sitting down from your belly, consider lying on the floor. Place a little book on your stomach and start relaxing so that the book grows as you breathe in and falls as you breathe out if you may want to listen to music that is calming as you practice deep breathing. DHRM Staff Welfare Division.

9.2 Relaxation Technique 2

Progressive muscle relaxation for stress relief Positive muscle relaxation includes a two-step process in which different muscle classes in the body are regularly activated and relaxed. Progressive muscle relaxing with regular practice offers you an intuitive experience with what pain, as well as total relief, you encounter in different parts of the body. Such sensitivity lets you identify and combat the first symptoms of stress-accompanying muscle tension. And so will your subconscious when your body relaxes. For an additional level of stress relief, you should incorporate intense respiration with gradual muscle relaxation. Many radical muscle relaxation practitioners begin at the feet and work their way up to the neck. See the box below to see a list of muscle groups to adopt. Lose your hair, take off your shoes, and make yourself comfortable. Relax, breathe in and out in long, deep breaths for a few minutes. Move your focus to your right foot when you're comfortable and ready to start. Take a moment to reflect on how it sounds — tensing the right foot muscles steadily, gripping as firmly as you can. Keep a list of ten. Relax the foot. Reflect on the fluid friction and the sound of your foot as it becomes soft and loose. Remain for a moment in this relaxed state, breathe slowly and deeply. Turn your focus to your left foot when you're full. Monitor and relieve the same chain of muscle tension. Slowly move through your body, contracting muscle groups, and calming as you go. At first, it may take some practice but aim not to tense muscles other than the expected ones.

The progressive cycle of muscle relaxation 1. Better foot* 2. Left leg 3. Third right bull. Calf 5 on the ground. Sixth right leg. Thigh 7 on the west. 8 Thighs and thighs. Stomach 9. Chest 10. Heart 10. Back 11. 12 The right arm and the right hand. 13. Right, hand, and shoulder. There are 14 back and arms. Face* alternatively, if you are left, you might want to continue with your left foot.

9.3 Relaxation Technique 3

Body scan meditation for stress relief:

A body scan is similar to cumulative muscle relaxation except that you actually concentrate on the sensations in each part of your body instead of tensing and relaxing muscles. Practice meditation on body scan! Lie uncrossed legs on your back, relaxed arms on your hands, open or closed eyes. Reflect on your breathing, making your stomach rise as you breathe and fall as you breathe out. Breathe deeply for about two minutes before you begin to feel relaxed and comfortable. Part of the worker's health of DHRM! Shift your attention to the right foot's toes. Note any feelings you experience when concentrating on your breathing as well. Imagine flowing to your toes every deep breath. Remain focused for one to two minutes on this area. Shift your attention to the right foot's heel. Change the sensations in that part of your body and visualize every breath streaming from your foot's sole. Shift your attention to your right ankle after one or two minutes and repeat. Transfer to your calf, knee, thigh, hip, and repeat the left leg series. Through the lower back and belly, the upper back and chest, and the shoulders move up the torso from there. Pay close attention to anybody area that causes pain or discomfort to you. Turn the attention to the right-hand fingers and turn to the thumb, forearm, elbow, upper arm, and shoulder. Repeat for the left arm. Then pass through your neck and chest, and eventually all the areas of your nose, the back of your head, and the top of your head. Take care of your mouth, chin, ears, tongue, nose, neck, hair, chest, temples, and scalp. Let your breath reach beyond your body as you reach the very top of your head and picture yourself hovering above you. Relax in silence and quietness for a while after finishing the body scan, remembering how the body feels. Then, gently open your eyes. Take a moment, if necessary, to stretch.

9.4 Relaxation Technique 4

Understanding for stress relief Awareness is the ability to remain conscious of how you feel right now, the perception of "moment-to-moment" — both internally and externally. Thinking of the past or worrying about the future can often lead to an excessive degree of stress. But you can get your nervous system back into balance by remaining calm and focused at the moment. Mindfulness can be extended to walking, running, feeding, or meditation practices. Awareness-giving meditations have long been used to relieve excessive tension. Some of these meditations bring you to the present by focusing your attention on a single monotonous movement, like your breathing, a few repeated words, or flickering candlelight. Many methods of meditation of mindfulness allow you to observe and then release your inner thoughts or feelings. Practice meditation on awareness! A quiet atmosphere. Choose a secluded place to relax without distractions or interruptions in your home, office, garden, and place of worship, or in the great outdoors. A convenient position. Get comfortable, but avoid lying down as it can cause you to fall asleep. Sit up straight in a chair or on the floor with your spine. You can also seek the position of a cross-legged or lotus. A focal point. This argument may be internal–a body part sensation or feeling–or something specific–a word or expression that you repeat during your session. With your eyes closed or open, you can meditate. Focus on an object in your world to increase your focus, or simply close your eyes. An observant mindset that is not serious. Don't think about disturbing your mind's thinking or how well you're doing. Don't fight them as thoughts come in during your relaxation session. On the opposite, turn your attention gently back to your focus point. Listen carefully! Consider yourself lying on your back or sitting in a comfortable position. When you sit down, be sure to keep you straight back and release the tension in your shoulders (let them drop). Your eyes are closed. Page of workers benefits for DHRM! Start by focusing on your breathing. Just pay attention to what it feels like to breathe in and out slowly in your body. Spend a couple of minutes concentrating your attention on the full breathing experience. Immerse yourself in this encounter absolutely. Picture your own breathing, "riding the waves." Once you've been concentrating on your breathing for some time, transfer your mind to your ears. Then let this knowledge spread from your ears and become conscious of all the sounds in your world and responsive to them. All you need to do is to be open to all sounds when they appear. Do not go in search of sounds or hang on to the sound experience. Alternatively, just practice getting a broad knowledge of all the sounds around you — near sounds, distant sounds, gentle noises, and loud sounds. Connecting work with the vibrations. See that you mark the sounds you hear (the "tick-tock" that I hear is from the clock on my wall, for example). If you label the sounds you hear, recognize this and then reconnect with the hearing experience and the sound quality (e.g., how loud it is or how long it lasts). Remember what brought you away from the present moment and bring your attention back to the sounds in your world if you remember that you are distracted by a thought (this is completely normal). Bring your concentration back to your breathing after a couple of minutes. Open your eyes when you're ready. Aware of eating! Choose a time and place to eat that helps to eat attentively. Try eating in a quiet environment free of distractions. It ensures that there is no food in front of the TV. Look down at your meal before you start eating. Consider what it looks like, how it tastes, and remember where it came from. See if you can catch the urge to eat before you take a bite (e.g., watering your mouth, feeling hungry). Place in your mouth a bite. Note how in your mouth the food feels and how it tastes. Note the things that happen in your mouth when you bring in food before you swallow. Remember how you are salivating; remember the desire to cough, note the chewing feeling. Remember what it sounds like when you swallow your food. How do you feel that your stomach is one bite fuller now? Repeat for each bite your careful eating before your meal is over. Try to decide when the meal is over based on your body's feelings (e.g., feeling full in your belly, feeling no hungrier) rather than whether your plate is clean. Attention to beginners! Look around your bedroom and locate an item you've had for a long time — something you know very well. It can be a hanging wall, a book, a plant, or even a garment. Sit down somewhere you can see your chosen object, close your eyes (if it feels comfortable), and take some deep breaths. Set your intent to cultivate the mind of the beginner. Open your eyes and look at your chosen object. Say you're from Mars, and you've never seen anything like that before. Look at the source, in fact, without judging it. Note the object's unique qualities. What's the feel of it? How does it feel? Where is it that catches shadows or reflects light? Continue to look at the object. Will you hear something you haven't seen before? Reflect on this exercise when you're done looking at the picture. Have you learned anything new about your chosen object? What would it mean if we could approach everything with the mind of a novice in our DHRM Staff Welfare Section? There are things, individuals, or circumstances that you seem to "automatically" respond to as if you already know what they are? Mindfulness of thought! Find a comfortable position, lying or sitting on your back. When you sit down, make sure to keep you straight back and release the tension on your shoulders. Let them go down. Your eyes are closed. Start by focusing on your breathing. Only pay attention to what it feels like to breathe in and out slowly in your body, focus your attention on the full experience of breathing for a few minutes. Immerse yourself in this encounter absolutely. Picture your own breathing, "riding the waves." Once you've been concentrating on your breathing for some time, turn your attention to your emotions. Bring awareness to any thoughts that come into your mind. Try to see your feelings as thoughts that are plain— just things in your mind, or events. Picture your thoughts as just clouds moving through the sky or leaves passing down a stream may be useful. Notice them enter, develop, and then float away in your consciousness. You don't need to check, hang on, or follow your thoughts. Let them arise alone and vanish. Each time you find that you get lost in thought (this is completely normal), remember what distracted you from your "observer stance" and bring your attention back to your thoughts consciousness. Turn your attention back to your breathing after a few minutes, and open your eyes when you're ready. Tips: It may be helpful first to develop a conscious awareness of your breathing before you attempt this exercise. O Make a habit of this. Practice daily. O Perform this exercise at first with not distracting feelings. Practice this exercise with other thoughts once you're relaxed. From time to time, you'll get caught up in your feelings. Try not to get upset— this is quite natural, and be mindful of this. Remember that this is normal when you get caught up in your thoughts and put your attention back to just analyzing your feelings.

9.5 Relaxation Technique 5

Visualization meditation for stress relief Visualization, or directed Visualization, is a twist on conventional meditation that allows you to use not only your visual sense, but also your sense of taste, touch, smell, and sound. Visualization, when used as a method of relaxation, means imagining a scene where you feel at ease, free to let go of all stress and anxiety. Choose the atmosphere that's most relaxing for you, whether it's a tropical beach, a favorite spot for children, or a peaceful wooded glen. You can do this visualization exercise in silence on your own while listening to soothing music, or a therapist's audio recording leads you through the imagery. You can download sounds that suit your chosen environment to help you use your sense of hearing— the sound of ocean waves, for example, if you've selected a beach. Visualization practice Find a quiet, relaxing place. During a visualization meditation, beginners sometimes fall asleep, so you may try to sit up or stand up. DHRM Division of Staff Welfare Close your eyes and let your fears go away. Picture your place of rest. Imagine it as beautifully as you can— all you can see, hear, smell, and sound. Visualization works best if you use at least three of your senses to add as many sensory details as possible. Choose images that appeal to you when viewing; do not choose images because they are recommended by someone else, or because you think they should be appealing. Let the photos of yourself come up and work for you. For example, if you're thinking of a dock on a quiet lake: Move around the dock slowly and note around you the colors and textures. Explore each of the senses for a while. See the sun setting across the bay. Hear the song of the birds. Smell the leaves of the pines. Feel your bare feet with the cool water. Feel the fresh, clean air. Enjoy the feeling of deep relaxation as you gradually discover your place of rest. When you're ready, open your eyes gently and return to the moment. Don't worry if, during a directed visualization session, you often zone out or lose track of where you are. It's usual. You may also experience fatigue or heaviness sensations in your muscles, slight, involuntary muscle movements, or even cough or yawn. Again, the answers are normal.

9.6 Relaxation Technique 6

Tai Chi and Yoga for stress relief Yoga, paired with deep breathing, requires a combination of moving and stationary poses. Yoga can also boost flexibility, strength, balance, and endurance in addition to reducing anxiety and stress. Practiced regularly, it can also strengthen your everyday life's relaxation response. The best way to learn yoga is to attend group classes or follow instructions on film. What is the best type of yoga for stress? While nearly all classes of yoga end in a pose of relaxation, classes that emphasize slow, steady movement, deep breathing, and gentle stretching are best for relief from stress.

• The traditional form of yoga is Satyananda. This features gentle poses, deep relaxation, and meditation, making this ideal for beginners and anyone looking for stress reduction in the first place.

• Hatha yoga is also a relatively gentle way of alleviating stress and is suitable for beginners.

• Power yoga is better suited for those looking for motivation and relaxation, with its vigorous poses and emphasis on fitness. Tai chi is a collection of slow, fluid body movements that are self-paced, non-competitive.

Such exercises emphasize concentration, relaxation, and intentional circulation throughout the body of vital energy. Although tai chi has its origins in martial arts, it is practiced today mainly as a way to calm the mind, strengthen the body, and reduce stress. Like in meditation, in the present moment, tai chi practitioners focus on breathing and holding their concentration. Tai chi is a healthy, low-impact choice for people of all ages and fitness levels, including older adults and injury-related people. Unlike yoga, you can practice alone or with others after learning the basics of tai chi or qi gong, tailoring your sessions as you see fit. How to Perform Yoga and Tai Chi the famous yoga and tai chi relaxation techniques benefit from preparation to ensure that the poses and movements are performed correctly. DHRM Staff

Welfare Section Making relaxation techniques part of your life, incorporating it into your daily routine is the best way to start and sustain a relaxation practice. Nevertheless, it can be difficult for many people to find the time between work, family, education, and other commitments. Luckily, as you do many things, many of the techniques can be learned. Rhythmic exercise as a technique of mindfulness relaxation Rhythmic exercise — such as running, walking, rowing, or cycling — is most effective when done with relaxation in mind when relieving stress. Unlike meditation, attention needs to be fully focused in the present moment, concentrating your mind on how your body now feels. When you exercise, concentrate on the physicality of the movement of your body and how that movement is complemented by your breathing. Gently return to concentrating on your breathing and movement if your mind wanders to other thoughts. For example, if you're walking or running, concentrate on each step— the feeling of your feet touching the ground, the sound of your breath as you move, and the feeling of wind on your face. Tips to match the strategies of relaxation in your life! If necessary, plan a set daily practice time. Set aside each day for one or two times. You will find that if you do it first thing in the morning, it is easier to stick to your practice before other activities and obligations get in the way. Practice methods of relaxation while doing other things. Try to breathe slowly while doing housework or office work that is not stimulating. Walking carefully can be achieved when you head to the office or as you climb the stairs at work. You can practice them in your classroom, balcony, space, or even bathroom once you have mastered techniques such as tai chi. If you are exercising, maximize the benefits of relaxation by taking care. Try to focus your attention on your body instead of tuning out or looking at a screen while you're exercising. If you're doing resistance training, such as lifting weights, concentrate on matching your breathing with your movements, and paying attention to how your body feels when you lift and lower weights. Do not exercise when you're asleep. Such methods can make you so comfortable that they can make you very sleepy, particularly when it's near bedtime. When you're fully awake and alert, you'll get the most benefit. Do not avoid using drugs, tobacco, or alcohol after consuming a heavy meal. I look forward to the ups and downs. When you miss a few days or even a few weeks, don't be discouraged. It's going to happen. Just start over and build up to your old momentum slowly.

Chapter 10: PTSD Therapies

10.1 Self-Therapy

Just as there is a wide range of different forms of psychotherapy, there are many different definitions of self-therapy. The term generally applies to psychotherapy that we can conduct on our own without a therapist's involvement or assistance (King et al., 2017).

Let's look at various terms that appear to use' self-therapy' interchangeably.

7 techniques on how best to do self-therapy Because there are so many different ways to do self-therapy–from CBT and Rational Emotional Behavior Therapy (REBT), IFS, and more, there are a lot of different tips on how best to do self-therapy. Here, some of the key things that contribute to better long-term outcomes have been extracted (Knaus, 2014; Therapist Support, 2018; Weiss, 2018).

Start by thinking about what you want to accomplish.

Would you like to master anxiety management techniques? Looking in the bud for nip negative thoughts? Would you like to focus on some constructive current behaviors? There is no answer to' false.' Clarifying your overarching goal would actually make it easier to grasp your various goals.

Understand your problem or target more.

Knaus (2014) explains how REBT includes separating the' question' into an emotional or behavioral component and a functional part. Weiss (2018) recommends learning more about your psyche's different' subpersonalities' that cause you problems. CBT techniques encourage the causes and cognitive biases to be established. All of these things have one thing in common. You need to improve your understanding of your problem in order to move towards your target. This article includes worksheets, questions, and links to resources that could be valuable starting points.

Research more closely, your thoughts, and/or habits.

Take a closer look at the presentation of your question. Would you like to deal with a behavioral problem, such as avoidance or coping behaviors? Or would you like to concentrate on unpleasant emotions such as social anxiety or stress? Studying your behaviors or emotions at a more in-depth level, they involve: Describing the feeling or behavior: what did you think, how intense was the feeling, and what else did you feel? Reminiscent of moments you thought or behaved in some way. Try to take an objective approach and remember where you were, who was there, and alternate acts or emotions you might have experienced; Keep a record of when and where certain feelings or behaviors pop up. Do you discern any patterns? Are there some circumstances leading to the problem?

Identify and discuss any self-talk, emotions, or opinions associated with it.

Very often, negative thoughts and actions are behind irrational or unhelpful cognitive mental processes. Stress, anxiety, depression, and even problems in relationships can often be resolved by recognizing the negative self-talk or contradictions in our minds. To direct you through this stage, please feel free to pick and mix any of the questions we have given in the next parts.

Challenge your emotions, internal debate, or convictions that are irrational.

We also included a selection of worksheets and resources to assist you with this move. The goal is to feel more positive, regardless of the direction you choose to take your self-therapy. We can do this much more effectively by treating the root cause of the issue, which is not done by many medicines.

Replace the thoughts or opinions that are irrational.

Sarah, for example, gets input from her supervisor on a work assignment. He replaces this with a more logical, rational thought instead of encouraging herself to think negatively (e.g., "I'm not good enough"). She says instead: "My boss sees my full potential, and I'm excited about -and realizing that potential."

Work, workout, and work.

We face threats and external events every day that we don't have any power over. When we practice, improve, and strengthen our processes of logical and positive thought, our reactions to them are better managed. To keep up the good work, reward yourself with something you enjoy doing.

10.2 Couples Self-Therapy

Self-therapy may seem like something that works only for individuals at first glance. In addition, for relationships, it is also quite useful. Couple therapist Toni Herbine-Blank has been counseling and treating couples with the IFS method for many years, and this approach will be incorporated in the article a little further.

How is it going to work? In short, we are taking the idea of internal conflict and applying it to our relationship dynamics. We accept that we are only human because we consider our own shortcomings and the contradictory dialogs within ourselves.

When we understand that, indeed, we can cure ourselves, we know that in our romantic relationships, the same thing is possible. We can also focus on our relationships in the same way that we can replace negative self-talk with logical and positive thoughts within ourselves.

Herbine-Blank wrote a more detailed article on couples ' self-therapy dynamics. Put another way: "The experience of caring for one's own inner family brings to the dilemmas of our spouse's empathic empathy and tolerance. Protective sections that formed earlier in life as a result of relational breakup slowly become less cautious and more comfortable. We build more empathy for other viewpoints with a good dose of self-love and loosen our grip of the need to be right. Our hearts are less secure. Differences are not a challenge to live with an open heart. "The Center for Self-Leadership blog will find her full article.

Use self-therapy for anxiety is part of anxiety's very existence. Triggers can be internal or external, and it is possible to get pretty quickly overwhelmed. As noted, not everyone can have immediate access to a psychiatrist, so directed self-therapy can be extremely helpful in dealing with daily occurrences that could lead to moderate or mild anxiety (Cuijpers et al., 2010).

How does anxiety work with self-therapy?

Self-therapy is often used as part of a type of stepped-care. This means that it is considered a treatment of low intensity that can be done without therapeutic intervention by people with anxiety. At the same time, practicing anxiety self-therapy will help us understand whether a higher-intensity approach is needed while being a useful tool to use in addition to one-on-one therapy (Gillihan, 2016).

There are different forms of self-therapy for work related stress and anxiety, including but not limited to (Cuijpers & Schuurmans, 2007): psychoeducation–tools to help you understand the essence of anxiety, and the vicious cycle of anxiety is often associated with worksheets, questions, and activities on self-therapy. We've provided some examples above, and these sheets also provide valuable information about what therapies you or your client might want to pursue; relaxation, of course, is a huge part of treating anxiety. Meditation, controlled meditation, music, exercise, and more can be part of self-therapy, and more exercises can be found to combat anxiety; cognitive reinforcement–the above' Challenging Negative Thinking ' exercise is a brilliant example of how cognitive biases can lead to anxiety, stress, and depression. The cognitive restructuring includes recognizing and modifying the mechanisms of ill-adapted thought that cause negative emotions and symptoms; anxiety reduction strategies–usually used in combination with cognitive restructuring and relaxation can include methods of self-therapy that function well in daily life. These may involve positive self-talking, calming strategies, and related exercises.

Depression self-therapy in a nutshell, depression self-therapy uses many of the same methods and strategies. Most depression self-therapy approaches use CBT techniques to identify, fight, and change negative thoughts. Individuals can easily learn to acquire cognitive behavioral therapy skills, and when self-directed, they can also help to reduce feelings of anxiety–as described above, both are often found together (Hirai & Clum, 2006; King et al., 2017).

Research on neuroimaging also provides evidence that CBT helps to reduce activity in our prefrontal self-referential medial cortex, which is typical' no' when we have negative self-conceptions (Yoshimura et al., 2014). There is a whole range of different activities linked to CBT that you can look at your own pace. OCD, Social Anxiety, and Self-Therapy because both social anxiety and obsessive-compulsive disorder (OCD) are correlated with anxiety symptoms, self-therapy is often used as a way to treat both. In reality, social anxiety is also associated with just under a quarter of those found to have OCD (Brown & Barlow, 1992).

In this scenario, self-therapy will often include discovering our psyche's nervous' sections' that cause obsessive thoughts, compulsive behaviors, or feelings of anxiety related to social circumstances. Social anxiety can often cause behaviors, particularly behaviors related to avoidance, and psychoeducation often starts with self-therapy aimed at treating it. In particular, research points to the effectiveness of cognitive-behavioral biblio-therapy and online programs for people with social anxiety (Furmark et al., 2009). Those results, even more encouragingly, showed signs of having continued a year later in follow-up trials.

The Internal Family Systems Model (IFS) and the Internal Family Systems (IFS) Model is a type of psychotherapy based on the concept of multiple subpersonalities in our psyches. Such multiple separate sections, which can be interpreted as painful emotions, reside within our mental structures and may clash with each other and with our spiritual core, the Self. Every subpersonality has a distinct set of motives, ambitions, thoughts, and emotions like' the angry part," the caring caretaker," the inner critic,' and more (Early, 2012).

IFS therapy, founded by Dr. Richard Schwartz, helps us to identify, target, and turn these various parts into inner strengths. (Schwartz, 1997) In other words, we should draw on the tools of power, affection, and freedom to deal with depression, anxiety, and other types of conflict between our' inner parts.' IFS ' ultimate goal in self-therapy is to engage directly with and restore these facets of our psyche to gain access to the Self, a source of inspiration, compassion, insight, and bravery (Scott n.d.).

According to the IFS model, through our emotions, perceptions, and physical symptoms such as anxiety and depression, we perceive our inner parts. Some are constructive, while others may be' exiled'–implying that they cannot play their intended role in helping you. Let's look at some of the inner parts that communicate within us, like how families or individuals connect in the outside world (Earley, 2010; Scott, n.d.): Protective inner' parts' The Managers–these constructive' organizer' aspects of our psychology strive to maintain equilibrium in our processes by keeping feelings associated with' exiled' parts under control. Elements of' Director' allow us to monitor our actions in different situations by minimizing threats and concerns, assessing ourselves and others, and related defensive behaviors.

The Firefighters–more reactive than' Managers,' these inner pieces are meant to distract you or dissociate you as they come into play from the displaced parts of your psyche. These can be felt physically as anxiety, hypervigilance, or related symptoms such as nausea and digestive issues. Exiles as detailed descriptions of Scott (n.d.) indicate,' Exiles' are young parts of the mind that for their own–or our–safety has become separated from the rest of our structures.

This separation may have been triggered by stressful, complicated, or painful experiences, and these sections hold the feelings and sensations of past experiences. If social influences or the method of IFS psychotherapy are used to reach these' exiled' pieces, they can cause us to feel extreme emotions in an effort to be understood and attended to.

10.3 Medication and Psychotherapy

Medication and Psychotherapy or amalgamation of the two, are the main treatments for people with PTSD. Everyone is dissimilar, so it may not work for another treatment that works for one person. To check out what works best for their symptoms, some people may need to try different therapies. It is essential for anyone with PTSD to be handled by a mental health professional who is familiar with PTSD regardless of what treatment option you select.

Psychotherapy Cognitive Behavior Therapy:

CBT is a form of psychotherapy that has been consistently found to be the most effective short-and long-term treatment of PTSD. CBT for PTSD is based on trauma, meaning the treatment center is the trauma event(s). It focuses on identifying, understanding, and changing patterns of thought and behavior. CBT is an intensive therapy that requires the patient practicing and learning skills to be applied to their symptoms at weekly appointments. The skills learned during therapy sessions are regularly exercised and help in reducing symptoms. Traditionally, CBT therapies take place over 12 to 16 weeks.

Key CBT components: Although different CBTs have different amounts of stimulation as well as cognitive strategies, they are the main constituents of the larger category of CBTs that have been shown to result in symptom reduction consistently.

- Treatment for touch. That type of intervention allows people to face and manage their emotions by introducing them in a safe environment to the trauma memory they encounter. Exposure may use mental visualization, writing, or visits to locations or individuals that remind them of their trauma. Virtual reality (creating a virtual environment similar to the traumatic event) can also be used to introduce the person to the environment containing the situation that is feared. Like other exposure methods, virtual reality can help with PTSD therapy experiences when the technology is available. Regardless of the method of exposure, in order to help them become less reactive over time, a person is often exposed to the trauma.

- **Mental reorganization.** This type of intervention makes bad memories beneficial to people. Individuals also recall their trauma differently from how it occurred (e.g., not knowing any aspects of the trauma, remembering it is a disjointed way). It is usual for people to feel guilty about aspects of their trauma that were not their fault in reality. In order to get a realistic perspective on the trauma, cognitive rehabilitation helps people look at what happened with reality.

What's the CBT? Hear this podcast.

It is essential for anyone with PTSD to be handled by an experienced PTSD mental health professional. And find out what works with their symptoms, some people will need to try different therapies.

Cognitive processing therapy (CPT)

Is a type of CBT that uses cognitive therapy to assess and alter trauma-related thoughts? Since witnessing a trauma, CPT focuses on how people view themselves, others, and the environment. Often after a trauma, distorted perceptions keep you trapped and hinder trauma recovery. Through CPT, you look at why the trauma happened and how it influenced the values of the victims. CPT focuses on learning skills to determine whether the facts support your beliefs and whether there are more effective ways of thinking about your trauma. Strong support for research shows the efficacy of CPTs across a wide range of traumas.

Long-term exposure (PE)

Is another type of CBT that focuses more heavily on behavioral therapy techniques to help people slowly resolve experiences, circumstances, and feelings linked to trauma? PE works on experiences to help people with PTSD avoid reminders of the trauma. Avoiding such reminders can aid in the short run, but in the long run, it will prevent PTSD recovery. PE uses fictional exposures that include recounting the nature of the trauma experience, as well as in vivo exposures that include frequent contact with trauma-related circumstances or individuals they have avoided in their lives. There is strong support for research showing the effectiveness of PEs across a wide gamut of traumas.

Eye Movement Desensitization and Reprocessing [EMDR] is a type of psychotherapy involving the retrieval of memories, thoughts, and feelings linked to trauma. When thinking about the trauma memory, EMDR tells people to pay attention to either a sound or a back and forth movement. The therapy has been found to be effective in the treatment of PTSD, but some research has shown that movement back and forth is not the active component of the treatment, but rather the stimulation alone. • Stress Inoculation Training (SIT) is another form of CBT aimed at reducing anxiety by providing coping skills to cope with the stress that may accompany PTSD. SIT can be used either as a stand-alone treatment or with other forms of CBTs. The main objective is to encourage people to react differently to their symptoms in order to behave differently. This is achieved by teaching various types of coping skills, including breathing retraining, muscle relaxation, cognitive development, and assertiveness skills, but not limited to. There is moderate support for research showing the efficacy of PEs across a wide range of traumas.

Some PTSD Treatments: Certain forms of PTSD are not known to be CBTs.

Present Centered Therapy (PCT)

Is a type of non-trauma-focused therapy that focuses not specifically on the trauma but on current issues? PCT offers psychoeducation on the effect of trauma on one's life and teaches problem-solving strategies for dealing with current stressors in life.

Psychologist Francine Shapiro developed a new form of psychotherapy called EMDR in 1987, which stands for Desensitization and Reprocessing of the Eye Movement. Over the past few years, EMDR therapy has become a more common treatment option for people with anxiety, panic, PTSD, or trauma.

"EMDR is an integrative psychotherapy technique that has been extensively researched and proven effective in treating trauma," according to the EMDR Research Foundation. EMDR therapy requires a series of structured procedures that combine elements from various approaches to treatment. EMDR has helped number of people of all ages to relieve many forms of psychological stress to date. "What is EMDR?

10.4 EMDR therapy

Is a gradual, centered approach to the treatment of trauma and other symptoms by re-connecting the client in a healthy and controlled manner to the trauma-related images, self-thought, feelings, and perceptions of the body and enabling the natural healing forces of the brain to work towards an adaptive resolution. It is based on the design that symptoms arise when trauma and other traumatic or stressful events trigger the natural healing ability of the brain and that the healing process can be stimulated and accomplished by simultaneous relaxation while the person re-experiences the trauma in the sense of the therapist's office's safe environment (dual awareness).

Dr. Romas Buivydas, Ph.D., LMHC, Vice President of Spectrum Health Systems Clinical Development, states the eight-phase treatment is EMDR therapy. "It recognizes and discusses traumatic experiences that have disrupted the normal coping capacity of the brain, resulting in traumatic symptoms such as hallucinations or anxiety, or unhealthy coping strategies such as alcohol or drug avoidance of actions and self-medication," he said.

How Does EMDR Work?

Individuals securely reprocess painful information by EMDR until it no longer disrupts their lives mentally. There are eight recovery stages, and the patient focuses on a destructive memory in the Rapid Eye Movement process and recognizes their confidence in themselves. If it is related to this negative memory (for example, when coping with violence, the person might think, "I earned it"), then the individual expresses a positive belief that they would like to have ("I am a deserving and good person in control of my life."). All the memory stimuli and feelings are described. The person then checks the memory while concentrating on an external stimulus, causing the bilateral movement of the head. This is typically done by watching two fingers pass by the therapist. The person is asked how they feel after each series of bilateral movements. This process goes on until the person is no longer bothered by memory. The trauma is being treated by the patient. Instead, by bilateral movement, the selected positive belief is built to replace the negative belief.

Usually, sessions last an hour. EMDR is theorized to function because the "bilateral stimulation" bypasses the area of the brain that retains memories because of the damage and prevents the brain from normal memory processing and storage. Individuals process the memory safely during EMDR, resulting in a peaceful resolution resulting in increased insight into both the previously troubling event and the negative thoughts about themselves that resulted from the initial traumatic event.

Who is using the treatment for EMDR?

The American Psychological Association and the International Society of Traumatic Stress Studies have approved EMDR treatment. This is also used by the U.S. Department of Veterans Affairs, the Department of Defense, and international agencies, including the United Kingdom Health Department and the Israeli National Mental Health Council.

According to the EMDR Research Foundation, there are now more than 30 gold standard studies documenting the efficacy of EMDR therapy over the past 30 years with issues such as rape and sexual abuse, combating trauma, childhood trauma and neglect, life-threatening accidents, and symptoms such as anxiety, depression, and abuse.

Edy Nathan, MA, LCSW, is a licensed psychotherapist with over 20 years of experience and qualified as an EMDR nurse, claims that this type of therapy has the ability to heal people suffering from the trauma of all sorts. "What the approach does is change the way we perceive the existence of directly traumatic event-related physical, emotional, and psychological effects," she said. "The pain and sense of danger brought into the self after a traumatic event capture the psyche with such purchase that it leads to a feeling of being in emotional fasts and. EMDR helps to disrupt belief systems, also known as cognition, and alters emotional perception through a sequence of lateral eye movements, tapping, or sound, while the client is asked to create the most disturbing picture of pain and threat (trauma)." Does EMDR Therapy Work Actually?

Some of the research on this form of therapy indicates, according to the EMDR Institute, Inc., that after just three 90-minute sessions, 84 percent-90 percent of single-trauma victims no longer have post-traumatic stress disorder. One research, sponsored by the HMO Kaiser Permanente, showed that after only six 50-minute sessions, 100% of single-trauma victims and 77% of multiple trauma victims were no longer diagnosed with PTSD. In another report, for 12 sessions, 77 percent of combat veterans were PTSD-free.

What's also unusual about this form of therapeutic intervention is that the therapist doesn't speak to the client during the process. Customers may have more vivid dreams after an EMDR session, may sleep differently, and may feel more sensitive to experiences or external stimuli. At the conclusion of each EMDR session, this is all shared with the client.

Conclusion

Post-traumatic stress disorder (PTSD) may affect many different people. This is a very common disorder, and many people tend to have this more than we may know these days. Each sign and symptom of PTSD may also be different from person to person. The signs and symptoms that may be present in someone who has this disorder may be reliving a horrible event through flashbacks, dreams or even nightmares. PTSD does not have a specific age limit but most men do seem to experience this disorder more than most women do. Psychological effects are very common within someone who has experienced PTSD. They are often reliving their traumatic experience within their memory. Treatments that have been proven to work for PSTD have been medication and psychotherapy. After reading all the efficient techniques and therapies to cope with stress and PTSD, a person has find the right type of medication and treatment that can work right for them.

References

Mayo Clinic. (2019). Post-traumatic stress disorder (PTSD) - Symptoms and causes. [online] Available at: https://www.mayoclinic.org/diseases-conditions/post-traumatic-stress-disorder/symptoms-causes/syc-20355967.

Verywell Mind. (2019). The Relationship Between PTSD and Other Anxiety Disorders. [online] Available at: https://www.verywellmind.com/ptsd-and-other-anxiety-disorders-relationship-2797549.

Verywell Mind. (2019). How to Reduce the Effects of Stress on Your Life? [online] Available at: https://www.verywellmind.com/stress-management-4157211.

Betterhelp.com. (2019). What Is Overthinking Disorder? | BetterHelp. [online] Available at: https://www.betterhelp.com/advice/personality-disorders/what-is-overthinking-disorder/.

Medical News Today. (2019). PTSD: Five effective coping strategies. [online] Available at: https://www.medicalnewstoday.com/articles/319824.php#10.

Verywell Mind. (2019). *7 Ways to Cope with A Crisis*. [online] Available at: https://www.verywellmind.com/cope-with-a-crisis-or-trauma-3144525.

Real Simple. (2019). https://www.realsimple.com. [online] Available at: https://www.realsimple.com/health/mind-mood/best-manage-your-anger.

https://www.goodtherapy.org/blog/four-steps-to-erasing-trauma-of-painful-memories-061214

Jayatilake, P. (2017). Mindfulness, Relaxation and Other Stress Relief Techniques. *Journal of Community & Public Health Nursing*, 03(04).

Adaa.org. (2019). Treatment for PTSD | Anxiety and Depression Association of America, ADAA. [online] Available at: https://adaa.org/understanding-anxiety/posttraumatic-stress-disorder-ptsd/treatment.

Lightning Source UK Ltd.
Milton Keynes UK
UKHW021017231120
373921UK00013B/1033